T0323696

Cambridge Elements ≡

Elements in Epistemology
edited by
Stephen Hetherington
University of New South Wales, Sydney

DEFINING KNOWLEDGE

Method and Metaphysics

Stephen Hetherington
University of New South Wales, Sydney

Shaftesbury Road, Cambridge CB2 8EA, United Kingdom

One Liberty Plaza, 20th Floor, New York, NY 10006, USA

477 Williamstown Road, Port Melbourne, VIC 3207, Australia

314–321, 3rd Floor, Plot 3, Splendor Forum, Jasola District Centre,
New Delhi – 110025, India

103 Penang Road, #05–06/07, Visioncrest Commercial, Singapore 238467

Cambridge University Press is part of Cambridge University Press & Assessment,
a department of the University of Cambridge.

We share the University's mission to contribute to society through the pursuit of
education, learning and research at the highest international levels of excellence.

www.cambridge.org
Information on this title: www.cambridge.org/9781009095136

DOI: 10.1017/9781009092203

First published 2022

A catalogue record for this publication is available from the British Library.

ISBN 978-1-009-09513-6 Paperback
ISSN 2398-0567 (online)
ISSN 2514-3832 (print)

Defining Knowledge

Method and Metaphysics

Elements in Epistemology

DOI: 10.1017/9781009092203
First published online: November 2022

Stephen Hetherington
University of New South Wales, Sydney

Author for correspondence: Stephen Hetherington,
s.hetherington@unsw.edu.au

Abstract: Post-Gettier epistemology is increasingly modalised epistemology – proposing and debating modally explicable conditionals with suitably epistemic content (an approach initially inspired by Robert Nozick's 1981 account of knowledge), as needing to be added to 'true belief' in order to define or understand knowing's nature. This Element asks whether such modalised attempts – construed as responding to what the author calls Knowing's Further Features question (bequeathed to us by the *Meno* and the *Theaetetus*) – can succeed. The answer is that they cannot. Plato's and Aristotle's views on definition reinforce that result. Still, in appreciating this, we might gain insight into knowing's essence. We might find that knowledge is, essentially, nothing more than true belief.

Keywords: Nozick on knowledge, Aristotle on definition, Socrates on knowledge, knowledge as true belief, defining knowledge

ISBNs: 9781009095136 (PB), 9781009092203 (OC)
ISSNs: 2398-0567 (online), 2514-3832 (print)

Contents

1 A Quest   3

2 An Hypothesis   7

3 Modalised Epistemology   14

4 Knowing's Further Features Question   22

5 Knowledge and Luck   30

6 An Aristotelian Strengthening of the Argument   34

7 Knowledge-Minimalism   47

   References   58

Preface

What is it to know a truth or a fact? Philosophers have long seen this question as having been posed by Socrates in at least two Platonic dialogues – maybe not only by him, but *importantly* by him. And an answer is *still* being sought. Why so? This Element will offer one reason why epistemology has made such scant progress on that front – and will suggest one way in which we might do better.

We will uncover a highly restrictive *methodological* mistake made by many epistemologists when trying to answer Socrates' question, when formulating theories as to knowledge's nature. Should we consider some competing forms of answer to Socrates' question? I suspect so. We can begin by expanding our sense of the *metaphysical* options. Specifically, might knowing, or at least its essence, be nothing more than *being correct in what one believes*? That is knowledge-*minimalism*. This Element takes a step towards endorsing it.

It is notable that epistemologists often regard these matters as initially arising, for Western philosophy, with those Platonic dialogues – but that almost no contemporary discussion of these issues holds itself *accountable* to those ancient writings. Is this because we assume that there is no real possibility that what we now say about knowledge's nature could need to *change* in light of what Socrates says? Perhaps. Yet that would be a mistaken assumption, as should become clear in what follows.

This Element will *blend* epistemology's Now with part of its Past. We need to learn some new lessons from those dialogues. And not only from them: Aristotle will also enter this story. (Plato and Aristotle are not the only ancient sources for aspects of contemporary epistemology. But they attract the most attention among current epistemologists, and I lack the space in this Element to travel more widely within the ancient world, such as by engaging with the Stoics and the Academic sceptics.) I will not contribute to strictly classical scholarship on ancient Greek philosophy. I draw upon it, though, in evaluating some current epistemology. In my experience, many epistemologists treat the issue of *defining knowledge* as a mainly modern concern, insofar as they are being 'purely conceptual'. Probably when teaching, and perhaps when introducing 'conceptual' discussions, they offer a professionally passing nod to Plato, always the *Meno* and often the *Theaetetus*, allowing that he made a solid start on this enterprise. For many, the next major 'conceptual' move was Edmund Gettier's in 1963, beginning our era of *post-Gettier* epistemology. I will argue, however, that Plato's relevance to this enterprise deserves more than a mere professional nod. Even while doing epistemology now, we should linger longer in Plato's company. His thinking about the natures of knowledge and of definition should make us wonder how well we have been approaching the challenge of defining knowledge. That moral is only strengthened when we invite Aristotle into the discussion, attending likewise to his views on the nature of definition.

Epistemologists have become comfortable with what, I will explain, is a potentially misleading formulation of what Socrates was asking when posing The Question that began Western philosophy's quest to uncover knowledge's nature. This Element's historical material invites epistemologists to revisit some of Socrates' thinking – and to be receptive to the idea that the contemporary project of trying to discover knowledge's nature should change in some vital respects. I will explain this in terms both methodological and metaphysical.

This will involve a focus on what we may call *modalised* epistemology. It might also be called post-Nozick epistemology, broadly considered, since its most apparent impetus was Robert Nozick's 1981 book *Philosophical Explanations*. It has been with us for almost as long as post-Gettier epistemology has been – which is since 1963, the year of Gettier's pivotal paper – and maybe much longer. Many philosophers thought that epistemology was taking a significantly new post-Gettier turn in 1981 when Nozick applied some bold yet delicate brushstrokes to Socrates' question and prior post-Gettier attempts to answer it. And in a few respects epistemology did alter direction slightly. Was that change enough, though? Not long after Nozick's book appeared, Richard Kirkham (1984) and Mark Kaplan (1985) described substantial cracks in post-Gettier epistemology's foundations. This could have lessened epistemologists' interest in post-Gettier thinking. But what happened was possibly a more happenstance shift of professional perspective: modalised epistemology looked interesting, as it started to form, to move, to grow. This continues, becoming more professionally attuned and technically accomplished.

Yet is that professional energy *progress* towards accurately answering Socrates' initiating question? I am not sure that it is, given this Element's argument. We begin by revisiting Socrates. We sit beside him. We listen to him. We learn from him. Then we rejoin our current world of epistemology with an improved sense of how to approach his question. It is not the only question, of course, with which we might approach epistemology. Nonetheless, it remains elegantly simple and motivational – and not yet as well-answered as we might think. My suggestion is that something of *methodological* moment has been lost between his time and place, and ours. We might have 'packaged' too swiftly the epistemological challenge that was set in those seminal writings by Plato, and we might still be doing so.

I urge a correlative pause, an informed doubt, a humble recognition of the genuine possibility that epistemology as currently practised is not where it should be, even in how it has conceived of the initiating challenge set for it by Socrates' question about knowledge, let alone in its consequent efforts to answer that question. I will offer a thought as to where epistemology *should* be, in its conception of knowledge's nature. That will be this Element's second theme, its *metaphysical* element – the knowledge-minimalism just mentioned.

1 A Quest

1.1 A Socratic Question

It might have seemed simple at the time. But the time in question was so early – the dawn, or maybe a few minutes later, of Western philosophy. It *was* the dawn of Western epistemology. The word 'epistemology' did not yet exist. Yet initial tentative epistemological steps were being taken.

And *what* was the 'it' that might have seemed simple at that time? It was this all-but-everyday question: *what is knowledge?* Presumably most people are confident, in an everyday way, of knowing this, or knowing that – of *having* knowledge, even of being able to describe the knowledge's content, what it is *of*. This is not the same as being able to describe what *makes* those instances of knowledge instances of knowledge. But (some will feel) how difficult could that be?

Many a person has walked into a Socratic web of doubt and hesitancy. To be fair, Socrates had a gift for encouraging others to be unwarrantedly confident in their answers to his earnest questions. One of those was the question of *what knowledge is*. This question arose for philosophers, for the first time as far as we know, most clearly in Plato's *Meno*, and, later, his *Theaetetus*.[1]

This Element begins, then, with a brief sense of how the question arose within those two settings.[2]

Meno. Near the close of this dialogue, we find Socrates conversing with Meno, seeking to know how 'good men' (96e)[3] are formed, those people who are so important to the just functioning of society, who 'give us correct guidance in our affairs' (96e). What does this require of them? Simply proclaiming

---

[1] The *Meno* is among what are often called *the Socratic dialogues*, interpreted as portraying the historical Socrates (Benson 2013: 136, 342 n. 1). Nails (2006: 4) apparently accords credence to the thesis that 'the dialogues with dramatic dates from 402 to 399 (especially *Meno, Theaetetus*, . . .) can be counted as sources for the kinds of conversations Plato, in his early twenties, experienced in the company of Socrates'. Prior (2006: 28) provides a dissenting interpretation: 'there is no decisive reason to believe that the dialogues [even] of the early group represent the views of the historical Socrates rather than an early stage of Plato's own philosophical thought'. Giannopoulou (2013: 2–3) puts the point thus: 'Since Plato wrote no history, he cannot be assumed to have recorded actual conversations. The Socratic dialogues are sometimes seen as hybrid constructs occupying the fraught area between history and fiction.' I will not engage with that scholarly issue. I use the term 'Socratic' as others have done, since this Element's focus is on how contemporary epistemologists have sought – but failed – to engage aptly with some ideas that entered Western philosophy in these dialogues, ideas advanced or evaluated by the 'character' Socrates – or, to again quote from Giannopoulou, by 'Socrates as the product of Plato's literary imagination' (3). On how to read Plato's writings, see Sayre (1995) and Corlett (2005).

[2] They are not the only Platonic settings that engage with this question or that point to the sort of answer that we will be discussing. See, especially, *Timaeus* 51e: 'we're bound to claim that knowledge and true belief are different, because they occur under different circumstances and are dissimilar. . . . the former is always accompanied by a true account, while the latter cannot explain itself at all' (translation from Waterfield (2008: 44)).

[3] I use Grube's (1981) translation of the *Meno*.

pertinent truths? Telling us what is, as it happens, correct? Is that enough? No. Socrates is almost emphatic (by his famously non-committal standards) in assessing this vital issue (97a): 'one cannot guide correctly if one does not have knowledge'. Unsurprisingly, Meno responds (97a) by inviting Socrates to develop this point further: 'How do you mean?' So, Socrates plunges powerfully into what is perhaps philosophy's initial epistemological moment, seemingly its first attempt to answer the question of what knowledge *is*. He is claiming that knowledge is needed in a truly good leader – someone with virtue, who can both embody and teach it to others. Within this, he is implicitly seeing knowledge as somehow *better* than ... what? What might we *mistake* for knowledge, if we have not thought carefully about this?

The answer arrives speedily. Socrates asks Meno to contrast someone 'who knew the way to Larissa' (97a) with someone who 'had a correct opinion as to which was the way but had not gone there nor indeed had knowledge of it' (97b). What advantage does the former have over the latter? To answer this is to point to what knowing provides, beyond what a 'correct opinion' does. It thereby tells us something distinctive of what knowing *is* – at least when knowing is compared to having a correct opinion.

And what is that 'something'? How are we to distinguish knowing from having a correct opinion? What marks, what signs, distinguish the former from the latter? Taking our cue from Socrates, we must seek an answer (98b): 'I certainly do not think I am guessing that right opinion is a different thing than knowledge. If I claim to know anything else – and I would make that claim about few things – I would put this down as one of the things I know.'

Again, then, how does knowing differ from having a 'correct opinion'? We return to this question in Section 2, when seeing how epistemologists have sought to do justice to the Socratic question with what has been seemingly the main *hypothesis*, about knowing's nature, flowing from the question. My immediate aim is preparatory, highlighting the Socratic question. Although many epistemologists insist that the hypothesis is pressing, irrespective of its historical roots, I will show (from Section 4 onwards) how such discussions can go awry if we do not maintain a proper focus on that initial Socratic question – and on something substantively constraining about it.[4]

---

[4] I follow the usual epistemological practice of interpreting Socrates' question as concerning a 'normal' form of knowledge. What other form could there be? McEvilley (2002: 186–93) highlights the idea that Socrates was at least sometimes focused on a 'special or yogic type of knowledge' (192). The links between some of Plato's writing here and some classic Indian philosophy are significant (187): 'sometimes it seems overwhelmingly clear that [Plato] is ... also including a higher intuition that might indeed be called mystical experience, trance, *samādhi*, and so on'. He gives us a 'distinction between changing and unchanging types of knowledge [that] is paralleled in many passages of the Upaniṣads' (188). This is an intriguing topic, but I will not stay with it here.

Theaetetus. The nature of knowledge is ostensibly this dialogue's topic. Epistemologists, however, generally attend only to its final ten or so Stephanus pages (201c–210c).[5] Like the *Meno*, yet in this case only after disposing of some alternative views of what knowledge might be, the *Theaetetus* asks how knowledge is distinguished from 'true belief' – 'correct opinion'. What are those discarded views? Swept along by Socrates, we swiftly leave behind, swirling helplessly in our wake, the theses both that knowledge is perception and that it is true belief.[6] The latter thesis, in Socrates' view, is easily shown to be false in a way that leads him, in almost a single breath, to asking what *is* enough, if true belief is not, for knowledge (201b–c):[7]

> when a jury is rightly convinced of facts which can be known only by an eye-witness, then, judging by hearsay and accepting a true belief, they are judging without knowledge, although, if they find the right verdict, their conviction is correct. . . . But if true belief and knowledge were the same thing, the best of jurymen could never have a correct belief without knowledge. It now appears that they must be different things.

What, therefore, is the difference? What marks the difference? What is knowledge, if not simply a true belief?[8]

---

[5] Even then, those epistemologists tend not to take into account the dialogue's seemingly being about knowledge of *things* (both concrete and abstract), not truths or facts. White (1976: 177–8) sees the whole dialogue in that light; Bostock (1988: 239, 270) restricts this reading to its second half, encompassing the *Theaetetus* pages with which we are most concerned.

[6] Some translations use 'judgement', not 'belief': McDowell (1973) does, while Cornford (1935) seems to use both (his Index entry for 'belief' directs us to 'judgment'). I follow Bostock (1988: 156): 'I have (for the most part) accepted McDowell's view that what Plato means to contrast with perception is *judgement*. But the Greek word in question . . . is more naturally taken to mean *belief* . . . and indeed belief is the more appropriate notion to compare and contrast with knowledge.' That fits well with contemporary epistemological interest in this segment of Socratic thinking.

[7] Here, and in what follows, *Theaetetus* translations are Cornford's (1935: 141).

[8] These two forms of question – the first seeking a mark of difference; the second focused on a general nature – will here be treated as functionally equivalent in their applications to the quest to understand knowing. Robinson (1971: 115–18) explains how both arise in Socrates' hands: 'many passages suggest that all he wants is a mark that shall serve as a pattern by which to judge of any given thing whether it is an X or not' (116).

> In many other passages, however, Socrates' purpose in asking What is X? is evidently not, or not merely, to distinguish X from everything else. It is to get at what he calls the essence or the form of X, the one in the many, that single identical something whose presence in all the many Xes is guaranteed precisely by the fact that we call them all Xes. (117; with an accompanying citation of *Meno* 74d)

I treat the two kinds of question as functionally equivalent, since they have been merged in practise by epistemologists: to describe the *mark(s)* distinguishing true belief from knowledge is, it has been assumed in practise, to do what needs to be done, and hopefully is enough, if we are to *define* knowledge, with its essence (if that idea has merit) being revealed.

1.2 A Philosophical Quest

Seemingly, therefore, Socrates bequeathed to us a significant question and potentially an inviting quest. Before trying to answer his question, we should note something of what made it a philosophical question, or at least a *Socratically* philosophical question. This determines what kind of answer is to be sought.

In one sense, this is easy to say: we are to uncover what knowledge is, our quarry being the correct answer to 'What is knowledge?' Yet complexities soon creep closer. For example, what *form* will that correct answer take? Here we must attend, certainly at the outset, to the Socratic slant on the question as it arose in the *Meno* and the *Theaetetus*.[9] We are setting out, with Socrates as our initial guide, to discover *what knowledge is*. What sort of discovery would this be? In particular, how metaphysical might our answer need to be? Some will wish to be less, not more, metaphysical. But this would not be true to the spirit in which Socrates posed his question. He apparently spoke with enough people, in a metaphysically sensitive way, that we can fairly (albeit inelegantly) claim that no answer would have satisfied him until it was revealing the nature of knowledge*ness*, or knowledge*hood*. Hugh Benson (2013: 136) says this: 'One thing we seem to know about Socrates is that he was preoccupied with questions of the form "What is F-ness?"'[10] In which case, to say *what knowledge is* was to say *what knowledgeness is*. Thus, it is natural to say that the Socratic aim is to understand (in whatever way and form this is possible) the *property* of being knowledge. This might include, or lead to, our understanding individual instances of knowing – in a specific way. We would be understanding their nature *as* knowledge. We would be understanding an individual instance of knowledge *qua* knowledge – its *being* knowledge, perhaps including its not being something else (such as mere 'true belief').

That is a metaphysical aspect of this Socratic quest.[11] We should also note a methodological or formal aspect, pointing to another Socratic *desideratum* via this question: can we find a *definition* that does justice to what it is to

---

[9] This will accord with how the question has helped to impart both form and substance to many contemporary examinations of knowledge's nature.

[10] But recall note 8: Socrates also approached this challenge indirectly, by asking about *marks of difference*. Robinson (1971: 110) says that what he calls Socrates' 'primary questions' take either the form 'Is X Y?' or 'What is X?' An example of the former would be our initial question, of how knowledge is different to true belief.

[11] I welcome these words from White (1992: 277):

> For some time philosophers have thought of epistemology and metaphysics as different branches of philosophy, investigating, respectively, what can be known and the basic properties and nature of what there is. It is hard, though, to see any genuine boundary here. The issues irresistibly overlap. Certainly in Plato there is no such divide. ... As a result his doctrines have a different shape from characteristically modern ones.

know – being sufficiently informative about what it is to know? Can we find a definition that describes knowing's distinctive nature? More fully, can we find a definition that describes a nature, for knowledge, that is *at least* distinct from that of a mere true belief?

It is common to regard Socrates as someone for whom the only form of understanding that would do justice to F-ness – the property itself, not merely instances of F-ness – would be a *definition*. The Socratic search is for a definition both insightful and full – a definition that neither wants for words nor wastes them. Did Plato follow Socrates in that quest? This can be debated (see Rowett 2018, especially chapter 5). But it is a sufficiently robust interpretation of Socrates, for my purposes. Even Catherine Rowett (2018: 26) tells us that, in the *Meno*, 'Socrates is not using definitions ... to stipulate or teach the meaning of a word, but that his purpose is philosophical, probably aiming to *answer* questions of conceptual analysis by presenting a successful definition.'

Let us remember this as we continue our investigation. Next, we consider the *content* of the attempted Socratic definitions, in the *Meno* and the *Theaetetus*, of knowing. (Then, Section 3 leaps forward two millennia, meeting anew that kind of definition, as it resurfaced within contemporary epistemology.)

2 An Hypothesis

2.1 A Socratic Version

Section 1 introduced Socrates' two famous moments of posing a question that helped to launch epistemology. Routinely, the word 'epistemology' is translated as 'theory of knowledge'. I prefer the term 'knowledgeology' (Hetherington 2019a: 13). But, in one way or another, attempts to answer our Socratic question – what is knowledge? – have been a recurring presence within epistemology. Before evaluating recent answers, though, it will be valuable to appreciate what ideas were offered by Socrates. (Again we consider the *Meno* and the *Theaetetus*.)

Meno. We met Socrates when he was posing his question, in the *Meno*, about how to distinguish knowledge from true belief. He was confident in there *being* a real difference. But what is it? How did Socrates proceed, in the *Meno*, to answer his question?

For he *did* offer an answer. This was not his usual practice. But epistemology was the winner. Philosophical interpretations can differ as to how we should interpret

---

In a similar vein, Gerson (2009: 11) highlights 'the assumption that epistemology is rooted in metaphysics'. He is discussing the ancient Greek presumption that knowledge has 'a distinct essence', a conception that 'is usually not [part of] the modern view'. Epistemologists have drifted away from talking of knowledge in that metaphysically intense way. As we will find, however, that might reflect *mistaken* moves within current epistemology. (Section 6.3 will discuss the most prominent such move, by Timothy Williamson.)

Socrates' thinking here. Still, there is a recognisable orthodoxy (be it correct, or not) among epistemologists as to what lesson Socrates sought to impart. What he supposedly taught to Meno was developed in a few stages, beginning thus (97b–d):

> as long as he has the right opinion [as to the way to Larissa] ... he will not be a worse guide than the one who knows ... So true opinion is in no way a worse guide to correct action than knowledge.[12] ... [Meno:] But the man who has knowledge will always succeed, whereas he who has true opinion will only succeed at times. ... [Socrates:] How do you mean? Will he who has the right opinion not always succeed, as long as his opinion is right? [Meno:] That appears to be so of necessity, and it makes me wonder ... why knowledge is prized far more highly than right opinion, and why they are different.

It then took but a moment for Socrates to proffer a view as to *what* that difference is (97d–98a; my emphasis):[13]

> Do you know why you wonder, or shall I tell you? ... It is because you have not paid attention to the statues of Daedalus ... [T]hey ... run away and escape if one does not tie them down but remain in place if tied down. ... To acquire an untied work of Daedalus is not worth much ... for it does not remain, but it is worth much if tied down, for his works are very beautiful. What am I thinking of when I say this? True opinions. For true opinions, as long as they remain, are a fine thing and all they do is good, but they are not willing to remain long, and they escape from a man's mind, so that they are not worth much *until one ties them down by (giving) an account of the reason why.* ... After they are tied down, in the first place they become knowledge, and then they remain in place. That is why knowledge is prized higher than correct opinion, and knowledge differs from correct opinion in being tied down.

What should we take from this thinking? I italicised the key move. Translating this phrase does admit of some flexibility, as suggested by this observation from Myles Burnyeat (1990: 240):[14]

> The Greek word *logos* also signifies reason, the faculty by which the mature human being is distinguished from children and animals which have only the power of perception (186bc). So why not suggest that each sense of 'account' picks out one function or group of functions that reason can perform? Articulate statement; definition, analysis, and classification; differentiation; justification, proof, and explanation – most of these can in

---

[12] This is an observation made also by Theaetetus when he returns, after discussing the nature of false judgement, to the hypothesis that 'true belief is knowledge. Surely there can at least be no mistake in believing what is true *and the consequences are always satisfactory*' (*Theaetetus* 200e; emphasis added).

[13] I say 'view' because Socrates describes himself as 'guessing' (98b), not knowing, the nature of the difference between knowing and true belief. In contrast, he claims (98b) to know knowledge's *being* different to true belief.

[14] In the same vein, see Cornford (1935: 142 n. 1).

suitable contexts be counted a *reason* for something, all of them can help us to gain knowledge and understanding both of objects and of true propositions about them.

Epistemologists have generally been content to take a specific moral from Socrates' picture. They standardly treat him as distinguishing between a *true belief* (*doxa*) 'on its own' and a true belief that has been tied down – tethered, bound – with a *logos* – involving, more fully, an activity of 'calculating' (to use Bluck's (1961: 412) translation), an *aitias logismos*. 'Account' is the standard English term used in translating the Socratic term. A fuller translation is 'account of how it is true'.[15] This 'how' is not what we now deem causal, detailing how a specific state of affairs 'entered' the world as a contingently produced consequence of something already present in the world. Rather, what epistemologists see as meant by Socrates is how we might fruitfully 'analyse' or 'explain' – thereby conveying an understanding of – what it is in the world that *amounts to* the state of affairs that is making the belief true.[16]

Imagine entering an examination, hopefully knowing truths that you will soon be writing on the examination paper. You open the questions booklet, and ... you have forgotten several of those truths. You know that you knew them, though. How can you regain them? Nothing guarantees your doing so. On the Socratic picture, however, your having *known* them includes your having had in mind a *logos* for each, and, so long as *that* has not been forgotten, you should be able to 'reconstruct' those truths, using one *logos* after another.

Conversely, if you *do* still have in mind a true belief, how do you make it an instance of knowledge? How do you impart to it a more secure status, in the sense of its not remaining vulnerable to being lost, departing your mind as an untethered statue by Daedalus will depart? The Socratic answer was clear, as far as it went: you add a *logos*; you hold on to *it*.[17]

Theaetetus. This time, the Socratic answer is less clear (and might not easily blend with the *Meno*'s): we end this dialogue without agreement on what a *logos* is if it is to mark the difference between true belief and knowledge. We may

---

[15] For more on translational subtleties encircling this, see Bluck (1961: 412, 413); Sayre (1969: 3 n. 2, 133; 1995: 228–31); Fine (1979: 366–7); Grube (1981: 86); Scott (2006: 179); Schwab (2015: 1); and Rowett (2018: 96).

[16] In more overtly Platonic terms, we may also understand this by adverting to the use of '*aitia*' in the *Phaedo* (100b–101d), where Socrates is discussing his 'theory of causation' (100b – Tredennick's translation, in Hamilton and Cairns 1961). By this, he means to be illuminating a thing's *formal* cause – how it is, once all has occurred to bring it into existence *as* this thing at all, *this* and not *that* F (for a kind F), hence *this* instance of the Form of F-ness. In this sense, these causes *are* the Forms (Sayre 1969: 7). Discussing the *Sophist*, Sayre says that 'The one Form . . . is the [*logos*] of the thing to be defined' (179).

[17] 'What *is* a *logos*? Does Socrates have an illuminating description of it?' Very soon, we will attend to details here.

wonder whether a *logos* is needed at all in order to distinguish knowledge from a true belief: the dialogue's 'attempts to define *episteme* [by using the term *logos*] fail, and no new model of how to proceed is on offer' (Rowett 2018: 170). Socrates considers three possible meanings of *logos*, rejecting each. The first asks for 'giving overt expression to one's thought by means of vocal sound' (206d). The second requires 'being able to reply to the question, what any given thing is, by enumerating its elements' (206e) – 'a complete analysis of a thing' (Giannopoulou 2013: 18).[18] The third is what 'most people would give: being able to name some mark by which the thing one is asked about differs from anything else' (208c) – 'a statement of the uniqueness of the thing known' (Giannopoulou 2013: 18). Have all possible meanings for *logos* been arrayed before us? If these proposals fail, must we discard the idea of a *logos* when trying to define what it is to know?[19]

Presumably not, given the meaning, albeit programmatic, for *logos* extracted so far from the *Meno*. We can briefly reinforce that optimistic thought, by lingering with the second and third suggestions.[20]

Socrates dismisses the second by focusing on the example of a word being analysed into its component letters and syllables, before envisaging Theaetetus as a boy, learning to read and write. As Cornford (1935: 158) says, on Socrates'

---

[18] Here we might be reminded of the 1942 poem usually called 'Naming of Parts', by the British poet Henry Reed, featuring this first stanza: 'To-day we have naming of parts, Yesterday, / We had daily cleaning. And to-morrow morning, / We shall have what to do after firing. But to-day, / To-day we have naming of parts. Japonica / Glistens like coral in all of the neighbouring gardens, / And to-day we have naming of parts.' Reed was capturing some of the analytic tedium in wartime service: the parts in question are a gun's parts. Socrates is asking us to consider *logos* as 'naming of parts' – 'itemizing all its parts' as part of knowing a wagon, for example (Sayre 1969: 134).

[19] Socrates' reasoning seems to move from (i) admitting that none of the attempts to define knowledge that he has considered, including his three attempts to use the idea of a *logos*, has succeeded, to (ii) this stronger thesis (Cornford's translation): 'So, Theaetetus, neither perception, nor true belief, nor the addition of an "account" to true belief can be knowledge' (210a–b); whereupon he apparently turns away from regarding 'the addition of an "account"' even as *needed* within knowledge. Epistemologists rarely, if ever, examine this idea; we will do so.

[20] A note on the first suggestion could be useful, though, if only to defuse incredulity at its presence, given how *clearly* inadequate it initially seems. It resonates with the philosophical element (341b–344d) in Letter VII, the Seventh Epistle. Some doubt this letter's having been written by Plato; others favour its being his. For discussion, see Morrow (1962: 3–17, 60–81) and Sayre (1995: xviii–xxiii), each of whom leans towards seeing the letter as Plato's. Certainly, *if* Letter VII was his, this adds interest to the first *Theaetetus* suggestion as to what a *logos* is, *if* a *logos* is to be a constitutive component within any instance of knowing. Letter VII includes an explanation (342b–344d) of why truly philosophical knowledge, at least, cannot be expressed, let alone conveyed, by words, either verbal or written. And this thesis about language and knowledge is far from trivial, true or not. As Morrow (1962: 12) says, 'if it were not the custom to ignore the letter, this passage [within it] would long ago have been regarded as of great importance for our interpretation of Plato's later theory of knowledge'. Cornford (1935: 169), too, seems to share such confidence: 'as we know from his Seventh Letter, Plato's final decision was that the ultimate truth could never be set down on paper, and ought not to be, even if it could'. For further comments in a similar vein (and definitely from Plato), see the *Phaedrus* (275c–276a, 277d), again on writing and speech.

behalf, '[T]he schoolboy may have a correct belief about every letter in the name "Theaetetus" and write it correctly, without having that assured knowledge which would save him from writing it incorrectly on another occasion.'

Socrates dismisses the third suggestion with an apparent dilemma (209a–210a). But I am unsure that we must accept his argument's first half (and the reason for this will be helpful in Section 7.2). Giannopoulou (2013: 19) succinctly renders his reasoning:

> Socrates rejects [the third suggestion] by claiming that a true judgment that picks out a thing from all others already registers the ways in which it is the same as and different from them. Therefore, if the account furnishes what the true judgment already has, it is redundant; if it supplies knowledge of the distinguishing mark, circularity ensues: knowledge will be true judgment accompanied by knowledge of the thing's difference from other things.

Ironically, Socrates' words point to a way in which we might remain attached to the idea of knowledge's including a *logos*.[21] He parses the third proposed meaning for *logos* as 'putting your differentness into words' (209a): 'the correct notion of anything must itself include the differentness of that thing' (209d). In which case, 'what meaning is left for getting hold of an "account" in addition to the correct notion?' (209d). Yet suppose that we see the third suggestion as complementing the second, in this way: (i) the second enumerates the elements constituting the thing being known (or constituting, if we persist in regarding knowledge-that as being discussed, the fact being known), and (ii) the third *highlights*, or *points to*, one or more of those elements, as distinguishing the thing (or fact) being known from other things (or facts) not thereby being known.

And of what might that combination remind us? We might usefully think of the ideas of *clarity and distinctness*, as Descartes explained these in paragraphs 45 and 46 of his *Principles of Philosophy* (Cottingham et al. 1985: 207–8):

> 45. ... I call a perception 'clear' when it is present and accessible to the attentive mind ... I call a perception 'distinct' if, as well as being clear, it is so sharply separated from all other perceptions that it contains within itself only what is clear.

---

[21] Without the interpretive suggestion that I am about to make, though, Socrates' words might point elsewhere (towards Section 7's minimalist picture). McDowell (1973: 257) says that 'the argument of this passage [Socrates' argument against the third suggestion] might well prompt the following thought: ... that true judgement concerning a thing already implies knowledge as to what it is'. Bostock (1988: 267) has a similar view: 'in effect the answer that Plato gives ... [is that] knowledge cannot be defined as true belief plus an account, because *some* knowledge is simply true belief and nothing more'. Gerson (2009: 54) sees that same reading but reacts differently (on Socrates' behalf): 'Plato's point ... is that if the addition of a distinguishing mark produces knowledge, true belief will already be knowledge. And that possibility has already been rejected in the dialogue' (at 200d–201c).

46. *The example of pain shows that a perception can be clear without being distinct, but cannot be distinct without being clear.*

Clarity is akin to a generalisation of Socrates' second suggestion for what *logos* could mean; distinctness is similarly analogous to his third suggestion. We do not dismiss distinctness as redundant, when pondering potential epistemic merits of a perception, merely because distinctness already encompasses clarity. Distinctness is, in effect, a way of *drawing attention to* the sufficiency of the clarity – to the content that is clear, in Descartes's sense. This can also be said, *mutatis mutandis*, on behalf of Socrates' third possible meaning for *logos*, as a way of being related to his second possible meaning.

Those comments do not do scholarly justice to the complexity in Socrates' thinking. I offer them in a conceptually conciliatory spirit, so that we need not feel compelled, by Socrates' apparent indecisiveness in the *Theaetetus* about what a *logos* is, to walk away from what is straightforwardly an embrace, in the *Meno*, of seeing *logos* as essential to knowing. At this stage, we may take from those dialogues a sufficiently united, albeit programmatic, commitment to the following hypothesis about a necessary element in how we would approach the challenge of defining knowledge by describing how knowing is more than having a true belief.

If a true belief is to be knowledge, it needs to be appropriately accompanied by a *logos*.

That is the schematic Socratic answer to Section 1's Socratic question as to what marks the difference between true belief and knowledge. The *Meno* pointed also to how we might make this less schematic:[22] even once one has a correct opinion, something more is needed; and this, suggested Socrates, is a *logos* – with his most apparently acceptable interpretation of that idea being the *Meno*'s, saying that a *logos*, as an account of a belief's being correct, tells us *what it is that amounts to* the belief's correctness. In what follows, this is what I mean when mentioning the Socratic idea of a *logos*.

2.2 A Contemporary Version

Have contemporary epistemologists followed that Socratic lead? No, in that they have not restricted themselves to using the idea of a *logos* when replying to

---

[22] If my earlier comments are correct, the *Theaetetus*, too, points to a way of making the story less schematic. We might also look to Sayre (1969: 213). Having called upon the *Sophist*'s (260a–264b) account of judgement (both true and false), he concludes that *logos*, in the *Theaetetus*, 'is the account concerning the object of judgment which exhibits necessary and sufficient conditions for its being what it is, thereby exhibiting the Forms which do and those which do not combine with its Form'. Epistemologists seem not to have noticed, and built upon, those possible interpretations. For argument's sake, I will work with the *Meno*'s account, as standardly parsed by epistemologists.

Section 1's Socratic question about knowledgeness. But yes, in that they have seemingly *generalised* on, or *abstracted* from, that idea, preserving enough of its spirit.

When asked about the philosophical lineage or pedigree for their efforts to understand knowledge's nature, epistemologists routinely mention Socrates' proposal in the *Meno*'s closing pages. But they generally eschew overtly Socratic *language* in their proposals. How *do* they claim to parse the lesson that they take from Socrates' reasoning, about what distinguishes knowing from having a true belief?

Here we move from Socrates' emphasis on the addition of a *logos*, welcoming what is either a generalisation of, or an abstraction from, his idea. A *logos* amounts to what epistemologists now call a kind of *epistemic justification*,[23] no matter that, as unfolds in the *Theaetetus*, we might find it difficult to say what a *logos* is. Unravelling the nature of epistemic justification is a substantial challenge. I take a small step here, then a larger one in the next section, towards conveying some standard thinking about it.

The small step is this: having a *logos* in mind, supporting the truth of a particular belief, is having in mind good *evidence* of that truth's obtaining. That is, we may treat a *logos* (in the form endorsed by *Meno*-Socrates) as a kind of evidence – this being our term, not Socrates'.[24] Recall, too, that I am working with the *Meno*'s sense of what a *logos* is – an account describing *in what it is* that the truth in question consists, or *how it is constituted as* that specific truth. Now reflect on how we use the term 'evidence': not all evidence need take the form of a *logos*, since not all evidence has the form of an account, in that *Meno*-sense. Some evidence points towards the truth's obtaining, like someone assuring one of a particular truth's obtaining but without also describing the 'inner structure' of that truth and how, specifically, it is 'fitting into' the world's larger complexity, say.

So, here is our initial expository step of building, in contemporary terms, upon the *Meno*-Socratic picture.

> What is also needed, if a true belief is to be knowledge, is that it be supported by *good evidence*.

---

[23] Or sometimes *warrant*, a term made popular for a while by Plantinga (1993a; 1993b). It amounted, in effect, to 'whatever, including any justification, is needed if a true belief is to be knowledge'.

[24] I use the term 'evidence' to convey what epistemologists will recognise as an epistemically *internalist* idea. Attending to the distinction between epistemic internalism and epistemic externalism – and reaching for developed instances of the latter, such as by allowing at least some epistemic justification to be constituted by facts about causality and/or truth-conditional reliability – is a feature of recent epistemology, not present in Socrates' thinking. For a simple explication of the difference, see Hetherington (1996: chapters 14, 15).

The evidence might be a *logos*; we would not spurn such evidence. But – looking beyond Socrates, stepping into current climes – we will not expect all evidence within knowledge to take the form of a *logos*. Thus, we gain a not-necessarily-Socratic hypothesis about what is needed for marking knowledge's distinctness from true belief.

Even so, will recent epistemology prompt us to move still further beyond Socrates' hypothesis? Is even the more general idea of evidence adequate for differentiating knowledge from true belief? This is what the next section begins to explore. In preparation, let us generalise, at least nominally and maybe really, this talk of evidence, moving to the idea of *epistemic justification* (whatever this involves) as needing to be added to a true belief if knowledge is to be the result.

> What is also needed, if a true belief is to be knowledge, is its being supported by *good justification, such as good evidence.*

So, imagine some good evidence accompanying a specific true belief. Is that enough to make the true belief knowledge? Is this a full story of the difference between true belief and knowledge? Do we now have a complete account of knowledge's nature – a definition of knowledge*ness* (as Section 1.2 called it, in a Socratic spirit)?

3 Modalised Epistemology

3.1 Post-Gettier Epistemology

Contemporary epistemologists are generally confident in their usual answer to Section 2's parting question. More specifically, post-Gettier epistemologists share that confidence.

We live in a post-Gettier time. Thankfully so, many claim, since it makes us heirs to a philosophical insight in Edmund Gettier's 1963 paper. Socrates said that if he knew *anything*, he knew that knowledge involves more than true belief (*Meno* 98b). Most epistemologists now agree that – courtesy of Gettier – if *they* know anything about knowledge's nature, it is that knowledge involves more than the specific 'more than' that Socrates added to the mentioning of true belief when attempting to describe knowledge's nature.[25]

So, our overview right now is brief. The basic tale of post-Gettier epistemology's coming into existence is long-familiar. The rest of this Element focuses on a substantial tale within that tale – what we may call modalised epistemology.

---

[25] Elsewhere (Hetherington 2016a: 2–3), I provide examples of how far that confidence has spread beyond 'specialist' epistemologists, amounting to a 'given' within contemporary philosophy. I quote from Lewis (1983: x), Glock (2008: 158), Bradley (2009: xiv), and Chalmers (2012: 13–15).

We meet it officially in Section 3.2. For now, I sketch lightly what an increasing number of epistemologists treat as a promising path of progress, still within post-Gettier epistemology as such.

I say 'as such' because not all post-1963 epistemology has been post-Gettier in the conceptual sense that matters to this Element: not all of it has *cared* about Gettier's argument, partly because not all of it aspires to describing knowledge's nature. But among epistemologists with that aim, Gettier's name is never far from their lips, in that they acknowledge his having *genuinely revealed* something of what knowledge is not – hence, implicitly, his having set in stone an unshakeable constraint upon attempts to understand what knowing is.

Gettier's professed target was the accuracy of a putative definition of what it is to have knowledge.[26] This is one reason why, in earlier sections, I charted carefully the Socratic path travelled towards either that definition or something close to it. Gettier (1963: 121) cited Plato – the *Meno* and the *Theaetetus* – when articulating his target. Here is Gettier's wording:

> S knows that P IFF (i) P is true, (ii) S believes that P, and (iii) S is justified in believing that P.

Upon this, he places two interpretive conditions (121) that need not detain us here.[27] Then he takes us immediately to two fictional stories that he sees as falsifying the sufficiency half of his 'IFF': in each story, we are invited to accept that there is a person, Smith, with a justified true belief falling short of being knowledge.

And that was that; except that it was only a start. Post-Gettier epistemology had begun – almost as soon as pre-Gettier epistemology was no more. Gettier's formative paper appeared; a philosophy-moment later, post-Gettier epistemology was upon us. Did Gettier establish what he claimed to establish – the falsity of the 'justified true belief' definition of knowledge? It seemed to most epistemologists that he did. Could we find a *better* definition, invulnerable to Gettier's form of attack? The fun was under way.

---

[26] He begins his paper by talking just of 'necessary and sufficient conditions' (Gettier 1963: 121), which he then formalises with 'IFF', before ending (123) by claiming to have shown the falsity of a 'definition'. In what follows, I talk of Gettier as engaging with a putative definition of what it is to know something: I treat his 'IFF as '=df'.

[27] We should note, given our earlier brief immersion in the Socratic thinking, that Gettier's term 'justified' seemingly adverted only to (epistemically internalist) *evidence*. We might add a detail to that, again with an eye on another distinction to which epistemologists have since become accustomed. One dimension of such evidence is its being *doxastic* justification, not propositional justification: the epistemic agent either is, or could easily be, *aware of using* the evidence, this being the sense in which her belief is being justified. For more on this distinction, see Carter and Bondy (2020).

What form has it taken? To chart and analyse its extensive hills and valleys would overwhelm this Element's allotted landscape. So, I will mention only passingly some of those more striking landmarks, before engaging with an increasingly influential style of response to Gettier's style of challenge.[28]

His immediate target was soon being called *the justified-true-belief definition* of knowledge. And his argument was soon treated by epistemologists as framing a further – still-continuing – challenge: please tell us what knowledge *is*, if not only a justified true belief. If the definition falsified by Gettier's two stories is not quite correct, with what should we replace it, so that we *do* have a fully and informatively correct account of what it is to know something? The post-1963 history of attempts to answer that question is often called *the Gettier problem* – the still-unresolved collective attempt to answer the definitional question about knowledge's nature that was given shape and urgency by Gettier's supposedly conclusive challenge to the justified-true-belief definition.

First there was the Socratic question – what is knowledge, if not merely a correct opinion (a true belief)? – along with the Socratic answer: knowledge is at least a true belief tethered by a *logos*. Then arose the post-Socratic *Gettieristic* question: what is knowledge, if not merely a true belief tethered by a *logos*? Or (to use Gettier's term) what is knowledge, if not merely a justified true belief? Thus was born post-Gettier epistemology, a still-continuing search for answers to that question, convinced that Gettier's critical conclusion was correct: what is knowledge, *since we are now given* its not being merely a justified true belief?

What have been the most influential kinds of answer, collectively giving form and substance to post-Gettier epistemology? We might note at least the following general kinds of suggestion arising within pre-Nozick post-Gettier epistemology.

- *Eliminate needless falsity* from one's evidence for a belief (if the belief is to be knowledge).
- *Eliminate ultimate defeaters* from one's circumstances – undefeated defeaters of one's evidence's being good enough support for a belief (if the belief is to be knowledge).
- *Eliminate inapt causality* from how one has formed a belief (if the belief is to be knowledge).

---

[28] For detailed presentations of that segment of epistemology's recent history, see Shope (1983), Lycan (2006), Hetherington (2011c; 2016a: chapter 1), and Turri (2019). It is possible that the basic idea behind Gettier's challenge also appeared centuries earlier, courtesy of at least Śrīharṣa in the twelfth century: see Matilal (1986: 135–7) and Stoltz (2007: 398–9); but see, too, Ganeri (2017: 523–4) for why a 'Śrīharṣa case' is not quite a 'Gettier case'. For another case, from the eighth-century Buddhist Dharmotarra, see Stoltz (2007: 398) and Williamson (2018: 50–3).

- *Eliminate unreliability* from how one has formed a belief (if the belief is to be knowledge).

Each amounts to a suggestion for how to render less schematically the Socratic idea of *something further* being needed if a true belief is to be knowledge. Each amounts to a way of trying to understand the kind of *justification*, broadly construed, that is needed if a true belief is to be knowledge. Each thus amounts (its proponents will argue) to the missing component in how we might be able to define knowledge so as to surmount Gettier's challenge.

Given the stakes involved, epistemological battles have been fought over those approaches. I have written at length elsewhere (Hetherington 2016a) about that history, including those post-Gettier ideas fast-approaching in Sections 3.2 and 3.3 – their chances of leading us to the post-Gettier nirvana of a full and frank definition of knowledge, a revelatory articulation of knowledge's nature. The argument in this Element, while partly descended from that earlier book's central argument, is new in at least two respects. It *highlights* modalised epistemology, from within post-Gettier epistemology. It is also new in its calling upon some ancient Greek philosophy in urging a halt to contemporary epistemology's modalised journey. The resulting argument will challenge both the methodological and the metaphysical cogency of a prominent strand in contemporary theorising about knowledge's nature.

3.2 Nozick's Account of Knowledge

Post-Gettier epistemology's continuing growth reflects especially modalised epistemology's still unfolding. Born mainly from Nozick's (1981) venture into such matters, it encourages us to enrich post-Gettier thinking with talk of possible worlds and subjunctive conditionals.[29] *Can* we meet Gettier's challenge in that way?[30] Nozick thought so, although he did not seek to *define* (or 'conceptually analyse') what it is to know. Still, he offered an 'account' constituted by 'conditions' that apparently function *as if* intended to be individually necessary and jointly sufficient conditions for having knowledge. And epistemologists have discussed these and descendant conditions in apparently the same spirit as they and their professional ancestors treated other conditions that have brought both fame and infamy to post-Gettier epistemology. Although his account's details

---

[29] Nozick was reaching for influential tools fashioned, a little earlier, by Stalnaker (1968) and Lewis (1973), in their analyses of the semantics, explicable by talking of possible worlds, of such conditionals. Less influential, but seemingly anticipating those analyses, was Todd (1964).

[30] Solving Gettier's challenge was not Nozick's only epistemological aim. Various shades of sceptical thinking were also, in Nozick's view, tamed by his account. I will discuss only his reaction to Gettier.

have received critical scrutiny,[31] significant aspects of the account have influenced much reflection on knowledge's nature. I will not delve into those details, in effect the periphery of Nozick-distantly-inspired modalised epistemological reflection; instead, something at such thinking's *core* will be examined. I will discuss an essential element of the general modalised approach, although I will do so, for specificity, by focusing especially on Nozick's account.

So, we need to have his account – his *tracking account* of knowledge – in hand. Here is a standard formulation.[32]

Someone, S, knows that p (for an indicative proposition 'p'), if and only if

1. it is true that p
2. S believes that p (while forming her belief by way of some method M)
3. if it were not true that p, then S (while still using M) would not believe that p
4. if it were true that p (in a variety of possible situations), then S (while still using M) would believe that p.

Conditions 1 and 2 are traditional (and will reappear, with surprising impact, within my argument). Conditions 3 and 4 were Nozick's distinctive contribution, the heart of what he called his *tracking* account:[33] *knowledge*, we are told, is *a belief that tracks the truth*.[34]

3.3 Further Modalised Accounts of Knowledge

Section 3.1 alluded to some strands of post-Gettier epistemology. We may also call them *Socratic* strands, since they suggest how one might render one's justification good enough if (with all else being equal) an associated true belief is to be knowledge. Let us now meet a few further such strands within Socratic

---

[31] For an early gathering of such discussions, see Luper-Foy (1987). More and more, though, his approach is used as a base for further thinking. Details, rather than its core, have been evaluated, as we will start seeing in Section 3.3.

[32] For fuller details, see Nozick (1981: 172–85).

[33] Those conditions were not as distinctive as Nozick *wanted* them to be (1981: 689 n. 53). Dretske (1970; 1971) had already formulated much of the same conception:

It grieves me somewhat to discover that Dretske also had all of this [what has been presented here, plus more], and was there first. It raises the question, also, of why these views have not yet had the proper impact. Dretske makes his points in the midst of much other material, some of it less insightful. The independent statement and delineation of the position here, without the background noise, I hope will make clear its many merits.

This has proved to be so. (But how marked *are* those 'many merits'? See Section 4.) For discussion comparing Dretske and Nozick, see Gunderson (2003: chapter 2).

[34] And, just as Alvin Goldman's term 'reliability' has become 'second-nature' epistemology-talk, the same is possibly true of Nozick's term 'track'. I suspect that many epistemologists now treat the question 'Does that belief track the truth?' as a way to begin or motivate an inquiry, not as a clearly technical locution.

post-Gettier (and post-Nozick) epistemology, ones that are increasingly visible within modalised epistemology.

- *Epistemic sensitivity.* Even if one has a true belief that p, would one (while using the same method, such as by retaining one's evidence for the belief's truth and using the evidence in the same way) have formed this belief even if p had *not* obtained – more precisely, even if the world had been different *only* (or as *close* to only as is possible) by p's not obtaining? Not retaining the belief that p within a relevantly possible not-p circumstance *should* occur, all else being equal. The alternative is that (while using the same belief-forming method, perhaps using the same evidence in the same way) one *continues* believing that p, no matter that one thereby has a *false* belief. If this might well happen, then one's true belief that p has not been formed in a way that is sufficiently *sensitive* to the truth that p; in which event, it is not knowledge.[35]
- *Epistemic safety.* Even if one has a true belief that p, how *stably* is one linked to the truth that p? That question, reflecting on the belief's (alethically) *modal* underpinning, becomes this: would one still have a *true* belief in other worlds as like this one as is possible, given that this likeness includes the same *belief's* being formed (via the same method, such as by using the same evidence in the same way as here)? In other words, would truth 'follow' one's belief across a range of worlds as like this world as is possible (with all else being equal, where one is using the same method, such as by using the same evidence in the same way, again to form that belief that p)? If this modal pattern does not obtain, then one's belief that p has not been formed in a way that is sufficiently (modally) *safe* in its reflecting of the truth that p: the possibility of its having been *false* (given the same belief-forming method being used, perhaps relying on the same evidence in the same way) is relevantly real; in which event, it is not knowledge.[36]
- *Veritic (epistemic) luck.* Can we fruitfully 'package' anew that idea of a true belief's needing to be formed safely if it is to be knowledge? Can we dress technical talk of epistemic safety in 'everyday' garb, emphasising its 'intuitive' appeal as a way to understand an element of knowing's nature? If so, we can 'transform' (i) the idea that a true belief is knowledge only if formed

---

[35] This is manifestly Nozick's condition 3, from a moment ago. For developments and discussions of it, see Roush (2005) and Becker and Black (2012).

[36] For a seminal proposal of this condition, an adaptation of Nozick's condition 4 (which itself is often called an *adherence* condition), see Sosa (e.g. 1999: 378). See also Williamson (2000: 123–30; 2009) and, still endorsing safety as an element within knowing, Sosa (2017: 57–62). The idea is gaining ground among technically inclined epistemologists, especially those writing within the shadow cast by Williamson's work: see, for example, Beddor and Goldstein (in press). I am sceptical (as will be explained in Section 6.3) about epistemology's needing to be reshaped along Williamsonian lines.

safely into (ii) a requirement that the belief's presence as a true belief has *not occurred too luckily*. What does 'luck' mean here? It has an 'everyday' veneer but remains technical, being epistemic luck – more specifically, veritic (epistemic) luck. It is epistemic by bearing on whether *knowledge* is present, thanks to the presence of a specific true belief. The luck is veritic in virtue of how the belief comes to be present as a *true* belief.[37]

- *Epistemically virtuous belief-formation.* Those three proposals (epistemic sensitivity, epistemic safety, and veritic luck) focus on the belief, its truth, how it has been formed (notably, the evidence supporting it and how that evidence is used), and other possible worlds. What of *the believer* at the core of that combination? What of her *as an epistemic agent generating* the combination? Do aspects of knowledge's nature reflect what it is to be an epistemic agent, 'standing behind' those other elements, 'turning them into' an instance of knowledge? Here we welcome *virtue epistemology* into the conversation. Roughly, we may parse its contribution along these lines.

  ○ To form a belief is to perform an action, or to do something enough like an action to admit of being *assessed* in some ways in which we assess actions.
  ○ What do those 'ways' encompass?
  ○ We can think of a *true* belief's being formed as relevantly akin to an action that has been performed *successfully*, in this respect: did the arrow *hit* its intended target?
  ○ We can ask whether the arrow hit the target from an exercise of *skill* or *ability* (as was intended). We can ask the same sort of question about a true belief's being formed.
  ○ Specifically, was the true belief (rather than a similar yet false belief) formed by exercising skills or abilities amounting, say, to a 'cognitive character'? Has this character properly motivated, controlled, and overseen the belief's being formed?
  ○ Now link that virtue-theoretic question with the modally substantive requirement that a true belief not arise in, for example, an unsafe way – a veritically *lucky* way – if it is to be knowledge.
  ○ We thus explicate, in partly modal terms, the virtue-theoretic idea that an element of a true belief's being formed by exercising a skill or ability (such as 'inner cognitive character') is that the belief, and its being true, has not arisen unsafely – veritically luckily. Real skill does not *need* such luck; and

---

[37] Epistemological talk of epistemic luck has become associated especially with Pritchard (e.g. 2005; 2007; 2008; 2012; 2014). Note Mylan Engel's (1992; 2011) early advocacy of it. See also Turri (e.g. 2011). Section 5 discusses it more fully.

knowing arises only via real skill, perhaps as part of an appropriately and sufficiently good cognitive character on the part of the believer.[38]

Thus, post-Gettier epistemologists have found it natural to explain in *modal* terms the first three of those four ideas as to what knowledge requires in addition to a true belief – the ideas of epistemic sensitivity, epistemic safety, and veritic luck.[39] Each can be parsed by talking of carefully corralled possible worlds. What of the fourth idea, the virtue-theoretic one? Obviously, it has long been motivated independently of Nozickean roots. Even so, it is naturally explicable in terms that owe much to Nozick's epistemological legacy: witness my speedy linking of it, a moment ago, with the idea of epistemic luck. And in sketching that possible linking I was reflecting what others have articulated more fully. Pritchard's 'anti-luck virtue epistemology' (2012) is one exemplar; another is his 'anti-risk virtue epistemology' (2020).

A further current instance of such a linking is Bob Beddor and Carlotta Pavese's 'modal virtue epistemology' (2020).[40] They preface their suggested account of knowledge's nature by acknowledging that, when surveying post-Gettier epistemology's skirmishes, we see that 'two [kinds of proposal] have emerged from the fray in relatively good shape, although not entirely unscathed. One of these is a *modal account*' (61). Which one? Of the possible ways to develop such an account, 'the most common proposal in the contemporary literature explains knowledge in terms, of *safety*' (61). What is the other main approach that they regard as a serious contender for what must be added to a true belief if we are to have an

---

[38] This extended story (in these indented paragraphs) is just one way to give voice to a virtue-theoretic conception of what is needed if a true belief is to be knowledge. For alternative and fuller versions, see Zagzebski (e.g. 1996; 1999; 2009: 124–9), Greco (e.g. 2003; 2010; 2012), Turri (e.g. 2011), and Kelp (2013). See especially Sosa (e.g. 2007; 2011; 2015; 2016), with his SSS (seat + shape + situation) modal conception of full competence. For a seminal doubt as to whether knowing is *so* strictly tied to the exercise of skill, see Lackey (2007).

[39] This recourse to modal terms, servicing that epistemological end, is an approach that I have also critically evaluated elsewhere (Hetherington 2017a; 2019b). Again, though, we should not forget how important to modalised epistemology has been the use of *conditionals*, such as in Nozick's conditions 3 and 4. So it was appropriate, when his account was championed by a popular 1980s epistemology textbook (Dancy 1985: chapter 3), to call it 'the conditional theory of knowledge'.

[40] Since I am highlighting their view as a representative instance of contemporary modalised epistemology, here is the view's core (Beddor and Pavese 2020: 73): 'a belief amounts to knowledge if and only if it is maximally broadly skillful – i.e. it is maximally modally robust across worlds where conditions are at least as normal for believing in that way', with this modal condition requiring the belief to be modally *safe* (70) – 'true in all of the relevantly close worlds' (Bogardus and Perrin 2022: 183). For an earlier linking of modal epistemology with virtue epistemology, see Kelp's (2013) requirement that knowing be 'safe-apt'.

instance of knowledge? 'The other major contender is virtue epistemology' (61). Hence I include it here.[41]

4 Knowing's Further Features Question

4.1 The Question

It is time to examine how well we can be guided by modalised post-Gettier epistemology *at all* towards accurately understanding knowledge's nature. I believe that epistemologists have misunderstood how to use such theories. I will illustrate that belief by focusing on Nozick's theory. But my criticisms will also apply, *mutatis mutandis*, to that theory's variants and descendants – indeed, to modalised epistemology more generally.

I begin with this epistemological datum, one with methodological bite.

> Any instance of knowing is *at least a true belief*. Without this combination being in place, no *further* features need be considered when we are assessing the presence (and thereby the nature) of knowing.[42]

---

[41] But I will not dwell on it; I have done so elsewhere. Beddor and Pavese say (2020: 61) that '[v]irtue epistemologists propose that knowledge is apt belief', such aptness being described by Sosa (2007; 2015). They introduce this resulting principle.

Aptness-Based Virtue Epistemology (AVE): S's belief amounts to knowledge if and only if it is accurate in virtue of manifesting an epistemic skill.

Here I mention one possible reaction to AVE (a reaction independent of this Element's argument). Elsewhere (e.g. Hetherington 2011a: chapter 2; 2017b; 2018b; 2020a), I argue that knowledge is always a kind of knowledge-*how*. For example, any instance of knowledge is a *skill* (2020a). More fully, it is a potentially complex skill on any given occasion of having the knowledge, and the capacity to form a cognate belief is one of the possible sub-skills collectively constituting the knowledge on that occasion. Having the belief is a possible way to *manifest* the knowledge-skill – that epistemic skill (to use AVE's term). The belief would not *be* the knowledge (even if it passes other epistemic tests); at most, it might be deemed the know*ing* (2011b). So, we can agree with AVE that agency matters in knowing. But we need not see a belief (even when epistemically augmented) as what *is* the knowledge. I mention this approach because it might be more palatable for some epistemologists than this Element's ultimate picture will be.

[42] Although this functions for almost all epistemologists as a datum, it has been questioned, as Nozick (1981: 680 n. 6) notes. I have done so (e.g. Hetherington 2011a: chapter 2; 2017b; 2018b; 2020a), through the idea in the previous note. Again, that heterodox account allows the *possibility* of belief's not being part of any instance of knowledge. On that conception, any instance of knowledge-*that* (our topic here) is an instance of knowledge-*how*. I call this a knowledge-*practicalism*: it sees all knowledge as practical in form, as knowledge *how to do* some (kind of) thing. Here, I set aside my practicalism; epistemology is a garden of many hypotheses, needing to be tested and encouraged in different ways. Still, it is worth mentioning this observation from Tiles and Tiles (1993: 11): '"*Epistēmē*" is a noun, derived from a Greek verb "*epistasthai*", which means "to know how to [do something]" or "to be capable of [doing something]". The traditional translation of "*epistēmē*" into English as "knowledge" tends to obscure the links which the Greek has to "know-how".' For discussion of the *Meno* and, given its concern with whether virtue is teachable, of what Plato means there by '*epistēmē*', see Bjelde (2021).

Nozick's conditions 1 and 2 are routinely regarded as jointly capturing this datum. (But we will find that care is needed even with this usual parsing.)

We may linger momentarily with that datum, in light of our earlier immersion in Socratic precedents. The datum standardly makes an early entrance when we introduce students to epistemology. Lo, there it is; whereupon students are invited to extract from it the following question.

> *What more is needed* if a true belief is to be knowledge? In what ways can a true belief *fall short* of being knowledge?

This is sometimes called *the* Meno *question*. I prefer a name that is less dependent on textual interpretation and that has fewer theoretical associations within existing epistemological writing.[43] I call it *Knowing's Further Features question*.

We may begin to clarify it by adverting again to Descartes's distinction between clarity and distinctness in an idea. Knowing's Further Features question's first half asks, in effect, for *clarity* as to what else, beyond truth and belief, is part of any instance of knowing (knowing-that, propositional knowledge). This would allow us definitively to *enumerate* any further elements within such knowing, beyond truth and belief. The question's second half, in effect, asks for *distinctness* in that same respect, so that we can definitively *distinguish* a true belief that is knowledge from one that is not.

Knowing's Further Features question has long been *the* initial question, it seems to me, posed by epistemologists inquiring into knowledge's nature. It is the routine prelude to being told something along the lines of 'Obviously, knowledge is always at least an accurate view, a true belief. But if the true belief is to be knowledge, it must also be justified or respect-worthy.' If any question 'kick starts' epistemological reflection within Western philosophy, it is this one. Introductory philosophy students might even encounter it in their *first* philosophy lecture.

4.2 *No* Further Features?

Nozick's conditions 3 and 4 are his answer to Knowing's Further Features question – his modalised answer. As we noted, many further epistemologists have sought to refine modally explicable conditionals, either Nozick's or related ones, that might articulate the right forms and strengths of truth-relevance for

---

[43] I have disputed (Hetherington 2020b), partly on textual grounds, the usual epistemological interpretation of this aspect of the *Meno*. But here I adopt the standard interpretation, since related standard *investigations*, built around this datum, are my target. I prefer to proceed, as far as possible, with those investigations' assumptions if I am to reach a critical result to which the associated standard ways of thinking must attend.

transforming a true belief into knowledge. It can be difficult to divert the path of a speeding train, maybe impossible. Yet I doubt that these excellent modalised epistemologists can be correct in their conceptions of knowledge, *given* a basic aspect of how they approach the challenge of understanding knowledge's nature.

That doubt begins with the following argument, framed for convenience in Nozick's terms.

Let TBp be a specific true belief that p, formed via method M by epistemic subject S. Consider what is needed in order for TB to satisfy Nozick's condition 3.

- 3 asks whether, if it had not been true that p, p would have been believed (by S, using M). Depending on the content of 'p', most epistemologists see this question as easily answerable: we need only do (as follows) what many philosophers have been doing for the past few decades, when calling upon supposed descriptions of various possible worlds.
- Thus, consider any possible world W that would standardly be deemed pertinent to answering our initial question. That is, consider any W from among the not-p worlds that are the most (among those sufficiently) similar to this actual world.
- Because (by hypothesis) W is a not-p world, it is automatically a world from which TBp is absent.
- For the record: if 3 happens to be satisfied within W, thanks to the *belief* that p being absent, then W is *doubly* a world lacking TBp. For my immediate purpose, though, this is unimportant. What matters is that we *already* knew that TBp was absent, simply by knowing that W is a not-p world.
- Why does the latter point matter?
- It tells us that W was never a world falling within the extension of the following description: 'a possible world where TBp fails to be knowledge, due to X, and/or a world where TBp is knowledge, due to Y' (with 'X' and 'Y' awaiting substantive details). W is not a TBp-world in the first place; hence, W is not a world where TBp, while present, fails to be knowledge due to some *further* feature.
- In short, W is not a world within a modally substantive footprint reflecting the travels – and possible epistemic travails – of TBp across modal space.
- This entails that W is not part of a story modelling modally significant behaviour of *the true belief as such* (TBp *qua* true belief) within other possible worlds. This is a direct implication of 3's requiring us to be assessing worlds from which, since they are not-p worlds (perhaps also not-belief-that-p worlds), TBp is absent.

- This matters greatly.[44] It entails that no worlds to which 3 directs us are ones *with which we can answer Knowing's Further Features question.* Within none of those worlds can we gaze *upon a specific true belief* and see *it* there as failing the further condition (beyond being a true belief) that is condition 3. No *true belief as such* is being seen to fail 3 within even one of those worlds.
- So, it is explanatorily pointless to call upon 3 when attempting to understand what, in addition to being true, is needed for a belief to be knowledge. This failing is one of methodological principle, present from the outset.

In Section 4.4, I describe a more general explanatory failing underlying this one. Already, however, a potentially powerful question arises. Might it be that no further features are needed, beyond a belief's being true, if it is to be knowledge? Maybe conditions such as Nozick's 3 and 4, not to mention more recent modalised successors, are beside the most important point in this vicinity. That 'most important point' is this: if those conditions, even in principle, from the outset, will be unable to answer Knowing's Further Features question, they fail to engage with what might be the clearest motivation for proposing them *at all* as describing essential aspects of knowing.

That idea is reinforced when we ask, in a similar way, what would be involved in applying Nozick's other 'further feature', his condition 4, to a specific true belief such as TBp. Again the accompanying reasoning is simple; again the result is not what epistemologists routinely say about knowing's nature.

- Let W be any possible world to which we are directed when applying condition 4 to TBp. W is thus one of those p-worlds that are the most (among those sufficiently) similar to this actual world.

---

[44] Or should we allow that reidentifying the same true belief in those worlds is not needed, because in any event – by reidentifying the belief, true *or not* – we will be discovering something about the belief's modal profile? The latter is true, but what we will discover is irrelevant to my immediate quest. Discovering that the belief need not be true, even when formed in the same way (via M), is one thing. Indeed, it is a fallibilist thing, hence of epistemic interest. But it is *merely* the fallibility of M. We are not thereby modelling a modal feature of *the true belief as such*, no matter that in this world M has produced this true belief. To see this more fully, consider why the following putative analogy fails (it is from a referee, objecting that my argument is too demanding): we can learn about 'the strength of a bridge by considering counterfactual circum- stances in which the bridge fails'. Yes, we can learn about the bridge's strength (as described modally) by noting how it reacts in possible settings, including ones where the bridge fails. Yes, by analogy, we can learn about the epistemic strength of *the belief as such* (that is, the belief, described *purely as* a belief) by noting worlds where it is present yet false. But we are not thereby learning about the modal strength of *the true belief as such* – which is what we are seeking to understand. Our Knowing's-Further-Features need is to model what else, *once it is true*, is needed if a belief is to be knowledge.

- What does 4 ask us to seek within any such W? What is being required of W by 4, if TBp is to be knowledge within our world?
- *Nothing* is being asked of W, in assessing whether it helps to make 4 true in this world, other than that it be among those sufficiently close p-worlds where that same true belief TBp is present (still via S's using M).
- We are assured that this is a substantive epistemological story. But is it?
- Gather together those worlds – this actual one, along with W1, W2, W3, . . . – that have, just now, been represented by W. Call this the set **W**tbp of those worlds whose collective existence amounts to TBp's satisfying 4. We will then be told that **W**tbp models TBp's satisfying, within this world, a *modally strong (enough)* condition on a true belief's being knowledge: the specific true belief that p is present in this p-world *and* in those other relevant possible p-worlds within **W**tbp.
- Yet *should* we regard that reading of 4 (or any other modalised condition very like it), as describing a substantive condition for knowing? I doubt it, since another way to present this dialectic is as follows.
- Suppose that we ask condition 4 to help us to answer Knowing's Further Features question. A methodological problem ensues. In setting out to answer the Further Features question, we *already* know that only TBp-worlds are being considered (since that question seeks to ascertain what, if any, further features *the true belief* that p needs if it is to be knowledge); in which case, 4 is empty, since we know *already* (given that we are working with what is presumed when asking that question) that our investigation will never be confronting a world that falsifies 4. We know *from the outset* that every possible world that could contribute to 4's being satisfied is one of those worlds – a TBp-world – whose *further* features we were aiming to find, with 4's guidance. So, 4's condition, when parsed as an intended answer to the Further Features question, is trivial. It adds nothing substantive to our quest to find what *further* features a true belief needs in order to be knowledge.

Once more, are we being led towards the idea that there is *nothing more* to a belief's being knowledge than its being true? This idea is rarely taken seriously by epistemologists; we return to it more fully in Section 7, after further preparatory argument.

4.3 The Further Power of Knowing's Further Features Question

The key to Section 4.2's argument is the methodological role – the procedural inescapability – of Knowing's Further Features question. As I mentioned when introducing it (Section 4.1), epistemologists use it readily in motivating their search for an account of knowledge's nature beyond 'Knowledge is at least a true belief.' The question's presumed appeal reinforces the feeling that there must *be* a fuller account of knowing. If this Element is right, however, that feeling might be misleading. Yet (most epistemologists will wonder) how *could* it be?

Think of how an epistemologist will usually apply a condition such as Nozick's 3. She attends to a roughly characterised group of possible worlds – those not-p worlds that are the most similar to this world (among those not-p worlds that are sufficiently similar to this one). She reflects on whether the epistemic subject S – mistakenly – believes that p within some of these not-p worlds. If she decides that the belief *is* present within at least some of them, she infers that 3 is failed. In which case, we are told that S fails within this world to know that p.

Now notice what is *not* happening within that foray into those worlds. Specifically, notice what is not being *re-identified* across them – namely, *the true belief as such*. Once condition 3 is formulated, we are asked to consider 3's satisfiability *on its own* – that is, *independently* of whether conditions 1 and 2 have been satisfied. We think that we can do this (as the previous paragraph described us claiming to do). But I explained (also a moment ago) why this is not a way of answering Knowing's Further Features question. It is not a way even of *asking* the question.[45]

That failure, presented here in terms of Nozick's conditions, has wider ramifications for modalised epistemology. It is a *basic* failure, endemic to a familiar epistemological method. That method proceeds by thinking along the following lines.

> Here are some conditions that are individually necessary and jointly sufficient for S's knowing that p: .... The first two of them (as with any set of putative conditions for knowing) are that S *believes* that p, and that it is *true* that p. Now let us examine the *further* conditions in that group: ....

But such thinking is misleading. Compare it with how the investigation should proceed:

> Here are some conditions that are individually necessary and jointly sufficient for S's knowing that p: .... The first two of them (as with any set of putative

---

[45] But (it was objected, by a referee) when we consider what question to confront, it is salutary to note that Nozick, at any rate, would want us to be answering the question of whether *the epistemic subject S* tracks the truth that p across relevant worlds – not whether S's true belief that p does so. Not quite. When Nozick (1981: 178) introduces his term, he says that it is the *belief* that tracks the truth in question. What I am adding is the detail that it should be the *true belief* whose credentials are being assessed, given the applicability from the outset of Knowing's Further Features question.

conditions for knowing) are that S *believes* that p, and that it is *true* that p. But we must not forget *the Further Features question*. Accordingly, we assume that those first two conditions are satisfied in this instance; whereupon we examine whether the further conditions in that group are *also* satisfied: . . . .

The latter method *presumes* that S has a true belief (since the Further Features question takes this presumption as a starting-point when asking whatever else must be present if knowledge is to be). The latter method then asks whether *that specific true belief* is satisfying whatever else must be satisfied if knowledge is present. The former method – the standard one – is not doing this, and hence is not even engaging with Knowing's Further Features question.

Already, that should sound worrying, as a verdict on the standard method. Speedily, it becomes even more so.

Suppose that, upon beginning another day of 'analysing knowledge', we remind ourselves that we are trying to discover what, if anything, is essential to knowing – knowledge's nature, in this Platonic sense of 'nature'. If we have a good day at work, we feel, we might find it – knowing's essence.

This section's argument might, or might not, be regarded as aiding that quest. We can also parse the argument's main result in this way: *if* Nozick's condition 3, say, describes a feature essential to knowing, *then* conditions 1 and 2 do not. For (as should be clear from the argument) once 3 is being applied, 1-plus-2 *is being set aside*: no world W that we are considering when testing 3 on its own is a p-world, let alone a TBp-world; on the contrary, to test 3 directly is to reach for a group of not-p worlds (before 'examining' them, for whether they are *not-believe*-p worlds). In practice, we are assured that this is unworrying, with epistemologists agreeing that if S is to know that p then S has a true belief that p (thereby satisfying 1 and 2) – whereupon we are told something like 'and now we are asking whether 3 is satisfied'. But we have seen that these epistemologists cannot thereby be saying 'and now we are asking whether 3 is *also* satisfied'. For, again, 1 and 2 cannot both be satisfied throughout, with this combination being held constant across those possible worlds to which the discussion of 3 directs us.[46] Given 3's antecedent, those worlds are not-p worlds. Hence, in none of them

---

[46] Someone might object to this (as a referee did), along the following lines.

> We are not obliged to *separate* these evaluations, of 1-plus-2 and of 3, say, as we ask what is involved in an instance of knowing. By analogy, suppose that your partner has always been faithful to you, perhaps while always living in Australia; even so, we can usefully ask whether, in a distinctive counterfactual circumstance (such as a visit to Siberia), he/she would remain faithful. In evaluating his/her faithfulness as such, we can – indeed, we should – at once take into account both of those kinds of assessment.

> The analogy is supposedly between the partner's being faithful and some belief's (even a true belief's) being knowledge. We can ask about 1-plus-2; we can ask about 3; then we can combine the results, due to seeking an overall evaluation (knowledge? not knowledge?). But the cases are

is 1 satisfied. Each such world is then 'inspected' for whether, within it, S believes that p – with 3's demand being satisfied within that world only if, within it, S lacks that belief. In which event, in no such world is 2 satisfied. Accordingly, there is a fundamental clash: epistemologists can defend 3 only by discarding 1-plus-2; conversely, to hold 1 and 2 fixed across worlds is to bypass worlds where 3's demand is satisfied. As I said, we thus see that the usual epistemological methodology here implies that *if* 3 is essential to knowing *then* 1-plus-2 is not. A possibly surprising choice must be made.

But it is not a difficult choice. This is part of the power of Knowing's Further Features question. The question's apparent inescapability tells us that, from the outset, we treat 1 and 2 as describing features essential to knowing. What *then* needs to be asked is whether further features are essential to knowing. My answer right now is that Nozick's 3, for a start, is not that sort of feature: epistemic sensitivity, in its Nozickean form, is not essential to knowing.

4.4 An Unwelcome Infallibilism?

Section 4.3's result is not a problem only for Nozick's sensitivity condition 3 – with 3 not being essential to knowing if 1 and 2 (truth and belief) are. For we can begin *generalising* that section's thinking, extending that result well beyond 3, as we contemplate modalised epistemology more generally.

Thus, once we hold in mind Knowing's Further Features question, we may set aside *any* condition that, like 3's construal of epistemic sensitivity, asks us to assess knowledge's presence by considering not-p worlds. This encompasses either (i) worlds that *are* not-p worlds, whereupon we would be considering whether they also include S believing that p (and perhaps other features), or (ii) worlds with an added feature (such as S's believing that p), whereupon we consider *whether* they are not-p worlds. Any worlds in (ii) that *are* not-p ones can, like those in (i), be set aside as unable to reveal knowledge's nature – given that we expect any such account also to be answering the Further Features question.

That implies a significant constraint upon the content of any conception emerging from those analyses. It tells us that Knowing's Further Features question cannot be answered in a way that allows for even the possibility – the obtaining within *even one* relevant possible world – of S's believing that

---

disanalogous. The partner can be evaluated without our holding constant that he/she is always in Australia. After all, he/she *could* have been equally faithful without ever having been in Australia. The belief, however, *cannot* be evaluated, for whether it is knowledge, independently of its being true. At any rate, this is so while we are recognising the methodological force of the Further Features question. If your partner leaves Australia for Siberia at some time, this changes nothing fundamental in any final evaluation of his/her being faithful. The analogous result is not available for a belief, insofar as we are asking whether it is knowledge: as soon as we are not presuming its being true, we have left behind a necessary condition of its being knowledge.

p along with its *not* being true that p: any relevant possible world includes both the belief and the truth. In effect, therefore, we would be able to derive only *a hidden or unwitting infallibilism* about knowledge's nature.[47] S knows that p only if S has a true belief that p; and if we proceed to ask *more* than this of S (seeking those 'Further Features' *while holding fixed* her true belief, to which they would then be affixed), before we can accord her knowledge that p, then we must infer that it is not possible for S, armed already with that true belief, to have the same belief along with its being false. This is part of the further power of Knowing's Further Features question, once we decide that knowing *needs* to include features beyond truth and belief.

Most epistemologists eschew knowledge-infallibilism. Few are sceptics about knowledge's existence, even while most accept that infallibilism is a wafer-thin step from scepticism.[48] Hence, what should they make of the present argument – the conceptual morass into which we might be about to step? At the very least, it might seem, *something* needs to be relinquished.

5 Knowledge and Luck

Let us focus on Nozick's condition 4 (since Section 4's argument was formulated mainly in terms of condition 3). Much modalised epistemology has welcomed a more, or less, close cousin of his 4 – some form of a *safety* condition, or, equally, of a *not-just-luckily-true* (or 'anti-luck') condition. Having introduced these ideas earlier (Section 3.3), I will now discuss them, especially the latter.[49] Its appeal includes its seemingly 'everyday' nature. Perhaps relatedly, many philosophers talk as if explanatory progress is achieved by imposing an 'anti-luck' condition upon knowing. But, we will find, Section 4's reasoning has exposed an underlying problem even for these modalised approaches: *they add nothing of explanatory worth*, once we are giving due respect to Knowing's Further Features question.

I will engage here with the basic idea behind such theories, a standard rendering of which is as follows. We are discussing someone, S, who forms a belief that p via method M. We ask whether S, within all, or almost all, possible worlds maximally similar to this one (given her still using M within circumstances as like her actual ones as possible), forms a *true* belief. She does so in this world, with her true belief that p; does she do so in all, or almost all, of those other relevant worlds? If not, her doing so in this world implies that *only*

---

[47] On how to define what it is for an instance of knowledge to be infallible, or, equally, fallible, see, for example, Hetherington (1999; 2016b), Reed (2002), Dougherty (2011), and Brown (2018).

[48] This is a very familiar conversation among epistemologists. For a recent discussion, focusing on Gettier cases rather than scepticism, see Anderson (2019).

[49] I will be brief. For more detailed critical discussion of anti-luck accounts of knowledge, see Hetherington (2014; 2016a: chapter 3; in press a; in press b).

luckily has she formed that true belief here by using M – in this modal-epistemic sense of 'luckily'. M has led her to a true belief that p when it might easily have resulted instead in a false belief.

But once we do methodological justice to Knowing's Further Features question, such anti-luck thinking should lose its appeal as a would-be explanation of a needed element within knowing. Here is why that is so.

- There are two cases to consider, if we are to understand the anti-luck condition.

  Either (1) the *belief* that p (formed by S within this world) is being evaluated across worlds; or (2) the belief-forming *method* M (which has led, within this world, to S's belief that p) is our transworld focus.

- That condition thus points to these two cases.

  Either (1*) in all, or perhaps almost all, relevant worlds where S, in the same circumstance, forms the belief that p, the belief is true; or (2*) in all, or perhaps almost all, relevant worlds where M is used by S in the same circumstance, a true belief is formed (which might, but might not, always be the belief that p).

- Now let us focus more fully on those alternatives in turn, *while also* holding in mind Knowing's Further Features question. In each case, what specific 'further feature' is being envisaged?
- Account (1*) directs us to a 'further feature' that, within each relevant world, is nothing beyond *the belief that p and its being true that p*. Yet an account's asking only for that array renders the account explanatorily pointless. Since Knowing's Further Features question *already* tells us that, within any world that we may consider with methodological propriety, we are evaluating from the outset the true belief that p, account (1*) *adds nothing of substance* about any world to which we are directed.
- Account (2*) has a similar failing. It directs us to a 'further feature' that, within each relevant world (or at least most such worlds), is nothing beyond *some* belief (maybe, or maybe not, the belief that p) and *its* being true. So, within any such world, either (i) the belief in question *is* the belief that p, or (ii) it is *not*.

  ○ For any instance of (i), (2*) collapses into (1*).
  ○ We must therefore focus on option (ii). On any instance of it, some *other* belief (not the belief that p) and whether *it* is true are what matter, as a result of M's being used, within the given world.[50]

---

[50] This might not even be the *same* 'other' (non-p) belief appearing time and again in those worlds. Within each world, M need only be issuing in *some* true belief – in W1 a true belief that q, in W2 a true belief that r, and so on. We need not add this extra detail to the argument.

○ And *how* should we focus on (ii)? As ever, we must not lose sight of Knowing's Further Features question.

○ Yet that (as I will now explain) is what this immediate proposal is in danger of doing.

○ That is because – in setting aside the requirement that within these other worlds S has (via M) the true belief that p – we are not modelling, across those worlds, the adding of a further feature *to the (true) belief that p*. Those worlds do not collectively model S's (*true*) *belief that p* being (a) re-identified across them and (b) having a propitious further feature. For S's (true) belief that p is *not even present within* all of them, on option (ii).

○ Instead, *all* that is being modelled collectively by those worlds, within option (ii), is M's having a transworld strength as a way to form a true belief at all – perhaps not a specific true belief (such as the true belief that p), but *some or another* true belief. And this, no matter its significance as a feature of M, is not modelling M's having that strength *along with* the true belief that p's being present. Hence, those worlds are not collectively modelling an answer to Knowing's Further Features question, as we have raised it *for* S's true belief that p.

Thus, such anti-luck accounts are 'talking past' the proper topic. At best, they are discussing something that is epistemically epiphenomenal, relative to the question of how we should answer Knowing's Further Features question. We may see this by applying the general form of reasoning from a moment ago.[51]

• Consider, again, an anti-luck epistemologist who says that S's true belief that p is not knowledge, *due to* arising in an epistemically lucky way via M. Something like the following 'further feature' is then said to explain that failing.

○ If S's true belief that p is to be knowledge, S must not have formed her belief by relying on a belief-forming method that has *only luckily* delivered this true belief to her.

○ S *avoids* that failing if, in all or maybe almost all worlds as similar to this world as possible where, in this same circumstance, she uses M, a true belief is the result (regardless of whether it is the belief that p).

• But here is why that account does not help to explain the putative fact of S's not knowing that p.

○ First, it is describing what would be a modal result only about M, not about M-*plus*-the-true-belief-that-p. This is because only the former, not the latter, is being *re-identified* across those worlds. That result might well

---

[51] Might any talk of luck, within epistemology or elsewhere, be illusory? Hales (2020) argues so.

be telling us that M – considered independently, on its own – is not guaranteed (or not even-almost guaranteed) to produce a true belief. That result cannot, however, be telling us that M – *when paired with* S's true belief that p – is not guaranteed (or not even-almost guaranteed) to produce a true belief. For, necessarily, there is no possible world where M, *paired with* S's true belief that p, is not producing a true belief.

- ○ And that limitation implies, given the methodological power of the Further Features question, that we cannot accurately describe M's modal-epistemic strength (as charted just now, with the true belief that p being set aside as we monitor M's 'travels' across those various worlds) as a 'further feature' contributing to S's belief's being knowledge. We cannot do so, that is, if we do not also hold in place, within our descriptions of those other worlds, M *plus* S's true belief. In short, on methodological grounds, what needs to be re-identified across those worlds is M *plus* S's true belief, not merely M. Only then are we modelling M's modal-epistemic strength *as helping to make* S's true belief knowledge.

- And so, just like that, discussions directing our attention to such phenomena as epistemic safety or epistemic luck, say, are beside the explanatory point – and are describing only what is epistemically epiphenomenal – since they do not do methodological justice to Knowing's Further Features question.
- The explanations that they have offered might be of M's less-than-stellar modal-epistemic strength, and so they can have epistemic significance, more broadly speaking. But they have one significant flaw, insofar as we might look to them when trying to understand what makes a true belief knowledge: they are not alerting us to a modal shortcoming of M-*plus*-true-belief – that is, of M *along with the fact of its having* led to a true belief.
- However, that is precisely what we need them to provide, if they are to explain why a specific belief, *even when true*, is not knowledge.
- Hence, those modalised accounts are non-starters as potential answers to the Further Features question, which *is* about how a true belief can become knowledge – and hence is about how a belief, *even* once true, could fail to be knowledge.

I hope that the moral from this section and the previous one is clear. When we aspire to understanding knowing's nature, modalised conditions like Nozick's 4 or even the anti-luck condition of epistemic safety, for example, offer us technicalities – *but no explanatory substance* – with which to enrich the initial truth-plus-belief condition set in place by an initial allegiance to Knowing's Further Features question. Such conditions are at best describing something that is *epistemically epiphenomenal*, as far as the presence or absence of knowing is concerned, for at least one kind of circumstance. What is that kind of circumstance? It is the presence of a true belief: *once a true belief is formed*, conditions such as those familiar ones *tell us nothing further* about what, if anything, makes that true belief knowledge.

6 An Aristotelian Strengthening of the Argument

6.1 Aristotle on Definition

Section 4.1 linked the epistemological centrality of Knowing's Further Features question to the seminal influence of Plato's *Meno*. Aristotle, too, can teach us about this issue. We should attend to his conception of *definition* – definition-by-division, or the method of genus-and-difference or genus-and-*differentiae*.[52] A definition – formally, a gathering of necessary and sufficient conditions – has seemingly been sought by most modalised attempts to understand what it is to have knowledge.[53] Unfortunately, however, they have paid little attention to Aristotle's remarks on such a quest. It is striking how readily applicable his thinking is to this element within current epistemology – and how easily, as a result, we might again doubt the efficacy of those contemporary efforts.

The general idea behind defining by calling upon genus-and-difference did not originate wholly with Aristotle. He was adding details and form to a heuristic advocated in some of Plato's thinking.[54] Each of Plato and Aristotle had their eyes on the prize of charting an epistemic path to knowledge of explanatory essences. But Aristotle sought to be more deliberate, with rules for constructing definitions adequate in that respect.[55]

- We identify a *genus* for S (the subject S of one's definitional quest).
- Next, in a carefully ordered way, we highlight two or more *differentiae* within that genus.[56]

---

[52] For that conception's details, see Aristotle's *Topics* (Book 6), *Posterior Analytics* (Book 2), and *Metaphysics* (Books 7 and 8). It is also called 'genus-and-specific-difference (*differentia*)'.

[53] Even when something looser than a definition is sought, such as an 'explication' or 'account', the fundamental elements of what I am about to say persist, *mutatis mutandis*. 'But what of Williamson's (2000: chapter 1) advising us to eschew conceptual analysis of knowing? Does his key argument evade my argument?' No, as Section 6.3 explains. I should also note that *conceptual* analysis need not be our quarry in this discussion. My aims are metaphysical, not conceptual, insofar as this distinction is achievable in philosophical practice.

[54] On this lineage for Aristotle's discussion of definition-by-division, see Deslauriers (2007: chapter 1). The lineage possibly included pre-Platonic seeds (12–14). Plato's thinking, upon which Aristotle aimed to improve, was his method of collection-and-division. We meet it in Section 6.4.

[55] See Deslauriers (2007: 19, 22, 26–9, 31–2) for how and why Aristotle sought to improve on details of Plato's method. See Sayre (1969: 186–92, 200–4, 222–3) on how the methods differ. See Bronstein (2016: 196–7) on Aristotle's aim being knowledge of essences.

[56] Why 'two or more'? This is a complex matter. For detailed reconstruction of Aristotle's thinking, see Bronstein (2016: 199–203).

That mention of ordering is deliberate. Although Aristotle talks of the genus-plus-*differentiae* collectively, he is clear on the need for an apt ordering to be manifest in the defining:[57]

> In establishing a definition by division one should keep three objects in view: (1) the admission only of elements in the definable form, (2) the arrangement of these in the right order, (3) the omission of no such elements. . . . The right order will be achieved if the right term is selected as primary, and this will be ensured if the term selected is predicable of all the others but not all they of it; since there must be one such term. Having assumed this we at once proceed in the same way with the lower terms . . . [W]e have taken the differentia that comes first in the order of division . . .
>
> the order in which the attributes are predicated does make a difference – it matters whether we say animal-tame-biped or biped-animal-tame.
>
> So, if we proceed in this way, we can be sure that nothing has been omitted: by any other method one is bound to omit something without knowing it.

The result should be a full and unified picture – unified, courtesy of the attributes listed and the order in which they are listed. It portrays what it is to be (an instance of) S, if S is definable in a way that will amount to knowledge. This is to be no arbitrary assigning of structure, through mere words, to a concocted concept. It is uncovering real essence, revealed in explanatory detail by the ordering's individual steps (again, if this is possible for S).

6.2 Aristotle on Definition on Nozick

What happens when we apply that Aristotelian schema to Nozick's modalised account of what it is to know?

- We begin by identifying the genus. Let this be *belief*.
- Next, we identify a first *differentia*. Let this be *true* – in contrast with *false*.
- Then we identify a second *differentia*. Let this be *tracking* – in contrast with *unstable or insensitive* (respectively, the substantive ideas behind not-3 and not-4). This *differentia* is Nozick's 3-plus-4. I cite this conjunction of conditions because Nozick does so when introducing his favoured term here – 'tracking'.

David Bronstein (2016: 199) has a helpful shorthand for what happens in such a case, when he describes Aristotle as 'establish[ing] by division that the essence of S is GD_1D_2'. Since the ordering is vital to that process, we may describe it more fully as Aristotle's asking us to uncover G-*then*-D_1-*then*-D_2.

---

[57] *Posterior Analytics* 2.13, 97a23–36, 96b31–2, 97a4–6. Translation by G. R. G. Mure (McKeon 1941: 177, 178).

The ordering matters, because Aristotle regards it as grounding the *unity* inherent within any genuine definition of what is fundamentally real. This unity is structural. The ordering reflects the identifying of a genus, for some S, followed by 'tiered' specifications of informative details for what it is to be S.

And Aristotle's picture blends smoothly with what we have independently uncovered in this Element. Applying the picture tells us that Nozick's conditions (as representative modalised ones) should not be treated as an *unordered* list. Instead, his account should be read as the ordered Belief-then-True-then-Tracking. This reinforces the role of Knowing's Further Features question: we had to presume Belief-then-True, *before* asking about the next *differentia* – which, for Nozick, was Tracking. Epistemologists have treated his account as, in effect, the unordered conjunction Belief-plus-True-plus-Tracking – this being the usual way in which epistemologists read accounts, such as Nozick's, as listing conditions supposedly needing to be satisfied if knowledge is to be present. We meet a conjunction of purportedly necessary conditions. We then evaluate each condition (such as Nozick's 3, or his 4) on its own as a condition for knowing. We do this with no apparent sense of the condition's being properly considered *only as* playing a role within *a properly ordered* set of conditions. Aristotle's schema might, or might not, be the final word on how we should approach such cases. But it is more subtle than what we find in paper after paper, book after book, of contemporary epistemology whenever conditions in the modalised spirit of Nozick's are assessed. Arguably, such epistemology has lost sight of what was potentially a real insight by Aristotle.

This Aristotelian point about ordering underlies (in different linguistic garb) Knowing's Further Features question's arising for attempts to understand the nature of knowing. Someone might reply that, in the final analysis, we are still saying that knowing that p is a matter just of having a belief tracking the truth that p ('a trackingly true belief that p'). She will claim that it does not matter in what *order* we list those components. She dismisses – perhaps as a superficial linguistic point – the Aristotelian moral that an account of knowing must not bypass the ordered genus-then-*differentia*-then-*differentia* structure – G-then-D_1-then-D_2. But her objection fails. This Element has shown (in effect, and on independent grounds) that the ordering is *vital* to what we can coherently uncover about knowing's nature. We derived this result while looking to Knowing's Further Features question. And now we may translate that earlier result into this section's terms, as follows.

If Tracking is our second *differentia* – as it needs to be, once Belief-then-True is the pertinent instance of G-then-D_1 – then the suggested Nozickean structuring, Belief-then-True-then-Tracking, will not be instantiated. After all, we have derived what amounts to this result: given Belief-then-True, we cannot coherently add Tracking as the next *differentia*.

This is a dramatic application of an ancient idea.

6.3 Defusing a Williamsonian Objection

But *should* we welcome that ancient idea, reinforcing this Element's conceptual argument? On the contrary (one might wonder), don't we have in hand a contemporary idea, thanks to Timothy Williamson, indicating how to evade this Element's thinking? Has our argument not been directed at an epistemological programme – pursuing an adequate conceptual analysis of 'knows' – that we could have set aside anyway, by looking to Williamson?

I am adverting to his currently influential knowledge-first programme – specifically, how it begins by indicating a supposed fallacy within epistemology's repeated search for a full list of necessary conditions on knowing. Accordingly, Williamson (2000: 33) urges us to eschew 'standard analyses' of the concept of knowing. Would this leave us with nothing illuminating to say about knowing's nature? Not according to Williamson, who seeks 'a modest positive account of the concept ... one that is not an analysis of it in the traditional sense' (33). In motivating this aim, he relies on some interweaving lines of thought,[58] the most immediately pressing being this (32):

> we already have the necessary condition that what is known be true, and perhaps also believed; we might expect to reach a necessary and sufficient condition by adding whatever knowing has which believing truly may lack. But that expectation is based on a fallacy. If G is necessary for F, there need be no further condition H, specifiable independently of F, such that the conjunction of G and H is necessary and sufficient for F.

In which case (some will infer), the project of conceptually analysing 'knows' was never philosophically mandatory. Hence (it might further be inferred), this Element's critique of how proponents of modalised epistemology have sought to analyse 'knows' may be bypassed, due to its engaging with what we need not regard as having merited such attention.

---

[58] For critical discussion of these lines of thought, see Cassam (2009). I will focus on what seems to me to be the strongest. It is not what Cassam (22 n. 7) regards as the strongest: 'the Inductive Argument is Williamson's best argument for' the Unanalysability Hypothesis about knowledge. The Inductive Argument is post-1963 epistemologists' failing to reach consensus on a definitional reductive analysis of (the concept of) knowing, in responding to Gettier's challenge to the justified-true-belief definition. That historical observation is far from decisive. I do not engage with it here, having done so elsewhere (Hetherington 2016a).

So, it is important to evaluate Williamson's reasoning. He ends the section containing that argument with the 'working hypothesis ... that the concept *knows* cannot be analysed into more basic concepts' (33). This hypothesis helps to ground his whole programme. But the inference leading to it is too speedy: Williamson overstates what, if anything, he has shown.

He overlooks another possible conclusion, one that coheres perfectly with this Element's story. He seemingly assumes (as most epistemologists do) that 'true belief' could not already *be* a complete analysis of 'knows'.

- Suppose we grant that Williamson's argument identifies an underlying fallacy in reasoning from 'True belief is necessary for knowledge' to 'Something further is also necessary for knowledge, something specifiable not in terms that themselves talk of knowledge.'
- I say 'underlying' because to describe that fallacy is to describe a possible instantiation of his more generically formulated argument. We need only instantiate his 'F' with 'knowledge', his 'G' with 'true belief', and his 'H' with the 'something further [that] is also ... '.
- The resulting reasoning impugns some epistemological thinking. But it might leave mine untouched. *If* true belief is all that is required, the fallacy highlighted by Williamson is irrelevant anyway.
- For all that follows from applying his reasoning here is that the *traditional* or *standard* ways of trying to analyse 'knows' are not adequately grounded, since, on those ways, we assume that there is more to knowing than having a true belief – that *this* is how we must answer Knowing's Further Features question.
- But we should be attuned, at this stage of the Element, to why that assumption is not inherent to the idea of conceptually analysing 'knows': it does not follow that analysis as such for 'knows' is ill-grounded. Rather, we have the possibility of ending the analysis with something like 'true belief' – *not* continuing the analysis by reasoning in the supposedly fallacious way identified by Williamson.

Williamson (2000: 33) begins his book's next section with what he apparently takes to have been established by his foregoing reasoning: 'Knowing does not factorize as standard analyses require.' We can agree *and* disagree with that. We can agree, by emphasising his term 'standard': knowing does not factorise as *standard* analyses require. But we need not agree by emphasising, as Williamson implicitly does, the term 'analyses': we need not deny that knowing factorises as *all* analyses require. So far, I have shown how, without needing to turn away from conceptual analysis, we might accept that epistemologists have standardly misused it. This does not entail a specific replacement analysis. But it leaves the door ajar. In seeking to answer Knowing's Further Features question, I have in effect argued, epistemologists carry the conceptual analysis further than they should have done, seeking an analysis that treats knowing as *more* than having a true belief.

I have not presumed the methodological health of conceptual analysis, even the project of conceptually analysing 'knows'. Still, I am content for the latter application to survive Williamson's attack, even if in the heterodox way mentioned just now. I am also happy to share *some* of his thinking: those traditional analyses of 'knows' are inadequate.[59] Williamson's argument is provocative, and it aids my cause here – contrary to what he would want. If only he had noticed that an analysis of 'knows' *need* never have been looking beyond 'true belief', he might not have embarked so speedily on his programme.[60] He might have felt a need to find a more substantial grounding for it.[61]

6.4 An Aristotelian Complication

Section 6.2 introduced us to Aristotle's genus-*differentiae* conception of definition. But we should note a complication. In *Parts of Animals* (Book I, chapters 2 and 3), he advocates a different structuring. His focus there is on biological classification, biological essence and definition. Do his *Parts*-remarks point to an alternative model for defining knowledge, one that evades my argument?[62]

The genus-*differentiae* structuring in *Parts* may be called *horizontal*. Picture a genus on one level, below which appears, on a single horizontal line, an array of its *differentiae*. The presence of each within that genus is assessed independently of the others. That is a quite different picture from what we applied earlier – in effect, a *vertical* way of arranging a genus and its *differentiae*. A genus is on one level; below it is a *differentia*; below *it* is the next *differentia*; below that is another *differentia*; and so on, as needed.

---

[59] Elsewhere (Hetherington 2016a), I have argued for this in detail, critically evaluating post-Gettier epistemology. Again, though, this story would take us needlessly far afield.

[60] It might be suggested that Williamson's view of knowledge, as (unanalysably) 'the most general factive mental state', is a way to treat knowledge in this way. Not so: his book (2000) proceeds to argue for knowledge's having many features – seemingly essential ones. He shows no sign of distinguishing some of these from others that are not. But this distinction, we will find in Section 7, does possibly apply here.

[61] Williamson might also have wondered whether, before definitively discarding the project of *defining* knowledge, due to post-Gettier epistemology's supposed failure to find a *conceptual analysis* of knowledge, it could be fruitful to revisit the Platonic roots for this entire enterprise. Might there be more methodological power to Knowing's Further Features question than Williamson (like many others) has noticed? I expand on this theme in the next section.

[62] This section results from David Bronstein's bringing these *Parts*-remarks to my attention and his framing the associated objection. The vertical/horizontal distinction is also his.

So, Section 6.2's Aristotelian argument was applying the vertical genus-*differentiae* definition for knowledge. This reflected the importance of Knowing's Further Features question, and it resulted in the ordered Belief-then-True-then-Tracking becoming the modalised (post-Nozick) definition being tested. On display was a genus, followed by a *differentia* 'below' it, then another 'below' the first one – all part of digging deeper with each step, uncovering knowing's metaphysically unified structure. That was the aim. But *could* we gain that definitional insight into knowledge's nature? No (I argued).

However, what of the horizontal form of Aristotelian definition, from *Parts*? Especially if we want knowing to be a *natural* phenomenon (a part of the natural order, probably the physical world), would we be better served by a definitional model arising in response to the unforgiving world of biological definitions? Can the horizontal model rescue the usual *form* of post-Gettier definitions of knowledge, with a genus *Belief* standing above a horizontal display of equally essential *differentiae*, each of whose presence within *Belief* can be established independently (in defining knowledge)?

We may link that question directly with Aristotle's *Parts*-thinking. On the vertical form:[63] 'Some people attempt to grasp the particular by dividing the kind into two differences. But this is in one respect not easy, and in another impossible' (642b5–7). He had doubts about that process of dividing, then again dividing, and so on (643b17–23):

> If one does *not* take difference of difference, one will necessarily make a division continuous in the same way that one makes an account one by conjunction. I mean the sort of thing that results by dividing animals into the wingless and the winged, and winged into tame and wild, or pale and dark. Neither tame nor pale is a difference of winged; rather, each is the origin of another difference, while here it is incidental.

We thereby have this picture (643b24–6): 'Accordingly, one should divide the one kind straight away into many, as we say.' In the terms used earlier (Section 6.2), instead of an ordered G-then-D_1-then-D_2, we are being encouraged to seek G-then-[D_1-and-D_2]. I focused on Belief-then-True-then-Tracking. Should we now accept the adequacy of asking only for the horizontal Belief-then-[True-and-Tracking], even accepting the methodological import of Knowing's Further Features question?

Here is how standard modalised-epistemology thinking might argue that we should.

---

[63] All translations here from *Parts of Animals* are by Lennox (2001).

- Knowing's Further Features question envisages our starting with *Belief*, then adding *True*, before we ask what else is needed. Equally, we might imagine responding with Belief-and-True, again before asking what else is needed.
- In either event, we have in mind a combination of *Belief* and *True* before continuing our inquiry. (For continuity with the earlier discussion, let us focus on the first combination.)
- What structured form must that inquiry follow? We have two options, the vertical and the horizontal.
- The vertical genus-*differentiae* form requires us next to move downwards, staying within the scope of our previous step – to *Tracking*, for example. (This is the path that we explored, critically, in Section 6.2.)
- But suppose that instead we now seek the horizontal alternative.
- Then we posit *Belief*, before posing, *independently* of each other, these questions: 'Must a belief be true if it is knowledge?' and (for example) 'Must a belief be truth-tracking if it is knowledge?'
- After which, still independently, we might find (indeed we will, according to many epistemologists) that the answer to each question is 'Yes'.
- Whereupon we may combine those answers, and the result is familiar: knowledge is (definable as) at least a true truth-tracking belief.
- We thereby evade the argument in this Element – another welcome result.

This is familiar fare (apart from its unusual Aristotelian garb). But it fails, as I now explain.

It is familiar fare because epistemologists often reason in that way. They might start with *Belief*, before adding *True* (gaining 'necessarily, knowledge is a belief that is true'); or, equally, they begin by putting in place Belief-then-True. What happens next? It is common then to focus anew on *Belief*, this time asking whether to add *Tracking*, for example. Prolonged epistemological debates ensue, maybe leading (within modalised epistemology) to a conclusion along the lines of 'necessarily, knowledge is a belief that tracks the truth', or, equally, the verdict that a definition of knowledge will include Belief-then-Tracking. And this will look like progress: 'So, knowledge is a belief that is true and truth-tracking.' But wait. This is where those same epistemologists routinely conjoin the results of those two independently derivable strands of reasoning, Belief-then-True and Belief-then-Tracking; which might well lead to their claiming that a definition of knowledge has at least this definitional structure: Belief-then-[True-and-Tracking]. Such reasoning is professionally standard, seemingly above methodological reproach.

But no, I say: it is only seemingly so.

- Consider any proposed examination of whether a belief must be truth-tracking if it is to be knowledge. We have found that this cannot be established *if* only true beliefs are being scrutinised from the outset, so that, strictly (and even if only implicitly), we are asking whether a *true* belief must be truth-tracking if it is to be knowledge.[64]
- That is a powerful result, since it reflects the apparent methodological priority of Knowing's Further Features question.
- Or is it? If this section's *Parts*-Aristotelian proposal is apposite, can we *cease* being beholden to that question?
- The *Parts*-proposal interprets the earlier limitative result as reflecting our search for what was the *optional* vertical form of genus-*differentiae* definition – and suggests that we can evade the limitative result by using the *horizontal* form.
- Yet that suggestion provides only a seeming reprieve. It can seem to reach its result that being truth-tracking is essential to knowing, *only* while 'setting aside' truth's being essential to knowing. This means that, in effect, we can infer the need for a belief's being truth-tracking only while treating truth as if it is *not* needed in knowing. This is unfair to the nature of knowing. We should not need to reason like that if we are to decide that *Tracking*, say, is needed within a definition of knowledge. Doing so renders any resulting allegiance to truth-tracking (as essential to knowing) false to an independently – and *even more* clearly – essential element of knowing. If anything is essential to knowing, truth is.

6.5 A Platonic Strengthening of the Aristotelian Strengthening

Part of this Element's thesis is that contemporary epistemology would profit from attending more closely to the ancient world for increased guidance on how to approach the challenge of defining knowledge. I have revisited Socrates and

---

[64] Again we might ask (as a referee did) whether my argument is too restrictive in its guiding thought. Why must we focus on the true belief, rather than the belief per se? I have answered this directly, in motivating my methodological focus on Knowing's Further Features question. But it is useful to consider another analogy (note 46 discussed one). When we evaluate S's moral responsibility for an action A, surely (if we do this in a modalised way) we take into account possible worlds where, with as much as possible held constant across these worlds, A does *not* occur. This tells us something about the measure and nature of the control with which S has performed A in this world. Is this the sort of evaluation that is present also when we ask whether S's belief that p, in this world, has been formed in a way that amounts to S's having the sort of control over, and identification with, the belief in order for S thereby to know that p? I reply by directing you to the metaphysical debate sparked by Frankfurt (1969) about moral responsibility and alternative possibilities, and especially to the response developed by Fischer and Ravizza (1998), with their emphasis on the 'actual-sequence mechanism' whereby an action has transpired.

Aristotle. The result has been a scepticism about a highly visible style of current inquiry into knowledge's nature. Taking our methodological cue from Socrates' guiding question about knowledge (giving us Knowing's Further Features question), before reinforcing that argument by applying Aristotle's conception of definition, we have found that modalised (post-Gettier) epistemology is methodologically flawed in how it conceives of even the *form* of an account of knowledge's nature.

We could wonder, though, whether Plato, apparently when moving *beyond* Socrates in his sense of how to seek philosophical knowledge, can rescue those same epistemologists. Does the ancient world display, with Plato, clear instances of philosophers attaining an accurate definition via what we call 'conceptual analysis'? Is Plato more apposite than Aristotle in that respect? When we formulate, test, refine, and replace a suggested definition – and then perhaps repeat, and repeat, and so on – are we following more the lead of Plato (or, at times, Socrates) than of Aristotle? May we therefore regard as irrelevant this Element's Aristotelian criticism of contemporary attempts to define what it is to know?

I am asking here about the Platonic method of *collection-and-division*. Is it similar enough to 'conceptual analysis'? Does Plato show how it can be used to gain an accurate definition? And is it sufficiently distinct from the Aristotelian method of genus-and-division, first finding the most pertinent genus, before dividing it, then continuing in that vein, as often as is needed?

Collection-and-division appears in some later dialogues – *Sophist* (253c–e), *Statesman* (285b), and *Philebus* (16a–17a), following its initial description in *Phaedrus* (265d–266b).[65] It is proffered as a path that can end with a definition, even of something subtle: *Sophist* finishes (268c–d) with a definition of what it is to be a Sophist, gained through a sustained application, and thereby an illustration, of this method.[66] Current philosophers do not describe themselves as practitioners of Platonic collection-and-division. But it might seem to accord with how they do describe their practice, since its quarry is what we would deem *necessary and sufficient* conditions, seemingly an explicative ideal for many. In our present case, we might see collection-and-division as a Platonic presaging of what post-Gettier epistemologists have been practising. Can epistemologists

---

[65] That is where the two procedures are first paired. As Sayre (1995: 149) notes, the initial mention of one of them, collection, is at *Phaedrus* 249c. He also suggests (Sayre 1995: 265 n. 24) that the combination appears in the *Theaetetus*, and is even (Sayre 1969: 55) presaged, to an extent, in the *Republic*. I concentrate here on the method's use in the *Sophist*.

[66] The *Sophist* also shows, early (218d–221c), how the method can deliver a successful definition of 'something comparatively small and easy' (218d) – an Angler. This is a 'lesser example, which will be a pattern of the greater' – namely, of the Sophist. (The latter translation is not Cornford's; it is Jowett's [1931]: see Hamilton and Cairns [1961: 960n].)

therefore fruitfully cite Plato, spurning Aristotle, as doing justice to how their attempts to define knowing *should* be modelled and then evaluated? Is collection-and-division a legitimising interpretation of current 'conceptual analysis' when a definition of knowledge is being sought?

Unfortunately for contemporary epistemology, the answer is 'no'. Before we see why, we should appreciate how collection-and-division proceeds. Here is Sayre's (1969: 177–8) description, parsing the Stranger at 253d–e of the *Sophist*.

> By whatever process, . . . an examination of several Kinds with a property in common serves as a collection if it exhibits that property as shared among the several Kinds. Thus the philosopher, in the process of collection, discerns the *one* Form . . . extended throughout the many . . . originally lying apart, and thereby comes to see the latter now as unified by the single common Form in question.
>
> . . . the philosopher turns next (perhaps again) to the process of *division*. He then attempts . . . to discern '*one* Form connected in a unity through many wholes, and *many* Forms, entirely marked off apart' [253d – Cornford's emphasis].

So, the *Sophist*'s central method 'involves the distinct procedures of discerning common elements in diverse forms of the thing to be defined and of articulating a formula specific enough to mark this off from all other things' (Sayre 1969: 224) – Forms within a Form. This 'exhibits conditions that are necessary and sufficient for being a thing of a given Kind' (Sayre 1995: 158). Thus, we have in hand a definition (Cornford 1935: 331 n. 1; Sayre 1969: 214)

Consider the *Sophist*'s parting picture (268 c–d), the Stranger's definition of the Sophist, manifestly a result of collection-and-division. I quote extendedly from Sayre (1969: 214–15), to make apparent one of the method's main aspects (one on which I will call when renewing my discussion of contemporary attempts to define knowing):

> At the beginning of this definition, . . . Art was divided into Productive and Acquisitive, and [the] Sophist . . . was pursued along the former branch. The distinction between human and divine production . . . is now made explicit . . . and within each class the further distinction is made between production of images and production of originals . . . . The originals of human production are the work of artisans and craftsmen, imagined in the arts of painting, rhetoric and sophistry. Image-making of the human variety then is divided again into the making of likenesses and the making of semblances . . . .
>
> Semblance-making then is divided . . . into production by tool and production, by voice or person, called 'mimicry'. Within the latter are further distinguished the productions of those, such as professional mimes, who know the subject they imitate, and those, like most public speakers on virtue,

who are ignorant of their subject .... The class of the ignorant mime is divided then into those who are simplistically unaware of their ignorance and those who are aware, but who through deceit are not thereby deterred .... The latter class finally is subdivided into the Demagogue who speaks at length in public and the Sophist who disputes in private. Thus the quarry of this unusually constructive dialogue is finally bagged...

I quote Sayre at length so that we appreciate the *sequential* – the organised *constructing* – nature of the collecting and dividing, the carefully ordered and layered way in which, actively, it reaches its final definition. That definition ends the dialogue; why was such a long journey needed? Indeed, why was a journey needed at all? Would it have been enough simply to present the definition in its entirety, reflecting a Moment of Insight by the Stranger? That is acceptable for current epistemologists, when seeking a definition of knowledge. But even if a definition is presented, and then discussed in a way that purports to explain and justify it, this procedure is not what Plato is demonstrating. The usual current approach is one of explaining the account, say, '*after* the event' (even after 'rationally reconstructing' the initial event) of actively developing the definition 'in front of a reader's eyes'. For Plato, though, the active ordering is of philosophical moment. He demonstrates *the defining*, in explaining and justifying *the definition*. Collection-and-division is a distinctive form of Platonic dialectic.[67] As such, it is an *activity*, having intellectual value *as* that activity. It enjoys an inner ordered structuring, too, and essentially so, one that helps to convey *how the definition is to be read* – namely, as *admitting of* being constructed in that way.

In this respect, the final definition, even once formulated (witness the *Sophist*'s final moment), is not detachable, in order to understand the thinking embodied within it, from the process generating it. As I said, *the definition* is inherently, and partly, *the defining* – which is itself the *giving of an account* (to adapt the Socratic phrase used earlier, in Section 2.1, when quoting from the *Meno*). In short, the defining is *the tethering* of a *logos* – in this instance, a *logos* offered by a philosopher seeking to understand what it is to be a Sophist. The *defining* is therefore, on the usual interpretation of what the *Meno* conveys about knowing's nature, necessary to knowledge being the result – in the *Sophist*, to *philosophical* knowledge (of what it is to be a Sophist) being the result.

---

[67] The term 'dialectic', as it arises for Plato's dialogues, seems to be used more, or less, carefully by different interpreters. I accept Sayre's discerning *three* forms of dialectical method as considered and used by Plato. There is a 'method of hypothesis', introduced in the *Phaedo* (100b–101e): see Sayre (1995: 137–45) for elaboration and evaluation. There is collection-and-division, as we are discussing. And there is what Sayre calls a 'new method [of hypothesis] employed in the *Parmenides*' (152), when Parmenides and young Socrates are struggling to understand the nature of Forms. For elaboration and evaluation of this third method, see Sayre (1995: 151–8).

We should now have a clear sense of the nature, and philosophical significance, of collection-and-division as a method of defining. It is time to revisit the objection, on behalf of contemporary epistemologists, with which this section began. My response is as follows.

For Plato, it would not be enough to offer a modalised account of knowledge that is simply a group of conditions – while ignoring *how that group should be constructed*, insofar as it is to be a definition providing philosophical (epistemological) knowledge of what it is to have knowledge. We need to model, as collection-and-division does, the defin*ing*, the *active generating* of that group of conditions, at least how it *can* be actively generated.[68]

This strengthens the import of an Aristotelian genus-and-difference approach, rendering the latter even more fitting when we evaluate attempts to define knowing. For the *active ordering* of the conditions matters. We should be treating the grouping of them as inherently modelling a 'rational reconstructing' of how they would have been *used*, actively and sequentially, to reach a definition – their respective sequential contributions to *an active defining* of what it is to have knowledge. Aristotle's genus-and-difference method differs from Plato's collection-and-division (see note 55). But they share this emphasis upon active sequencing – a feature sufficient to undermine the objection now being discussed (which proposed moving away from Aristotelian genus-and-difference, towards Platonic collection-and-division).

That reinforces the rightness of how we have focused on Knowing's Further Features question and its methodological import, when striving to build upon Socrates' supposed insight that knowledge is more than mere true belief, and to answer his correlative question of what knowledge is, if not merely true belief. That question should be interpreted as part of seeking a *sequentially active* definition of knowing, servicing either genus-and-difference or collection-and-division. We begin with the idea of knowledge's being at least true belief, before wondering what is to be added to that idea; after which (we continue), perhaps

---

[68] At least, we do, *if* we are working with a methodology historically indebted to Plato and Knowing's Further Features question. Should we turn our backs on that past? What alternative methodologies are available? Answering this more fully will take us too far afield. Nonetheless, we *might* say (as a referee did) that epistemologists often proceed in a non-Platonic and non-Aristotelian way, by proposing general epistemic theses in order to test them with putative counterexamples. Yet is that so different to how Socrates works his *aporetic* magic? We might think so, by deeming that description to be both Chisholmian and Popperian – the former due to the repeated fine-tuning of epistemic theses with subtle counterexamples, the latter due to the idea of trying to falsify a theory. Still in a Popperian spirit, we might then be fallibilist by only-provisionally accepting any post-counterexample epistemic theory left standing. This fallibilism is not clearly Platonic. But it is Socratic. And we might readily regard Knowing's Further Features question as implicitly presenting us with an epistemic principle – that knowing is true belief *and maybe more* – which we are then testing, maybe along the lines in this Element.

something further is to be added; and so on. That sounds comfortingly familiar, seemingly saying nothing more than that – quite aptly – we begin with what will be *only part* of the final definition; then we start building upon that initial step, always holding it in place as we consider further conditions that we might see as being needed. But we have found that even this familiar picture must be handled with new care, since closer inspection of its contents might reveal something less familiar, even confronting.

Indeed, that has been occurring. *Can* we discover Knowing's Further Features? Not within modalised epistemology, for a start, given its conceptual analyses. Must we follow Williamson, instead, in eschewing conceptual analysis? No, because (in standard fashion) he has simply *presumed* that knowing has Further Features. And might that presumption itself be mistaken? Might knowing *lack* Further Features? Might *this* be the answer, even if surprisingly so, to Knowing's Further Features question?

7 Knowledge-Minimalism

7.1 Might It Be True?

Epistemologists in general recoil from defining knowledge merely as true belief. *Is* that even a conception of knowledge (many will ask)?

I believe so. I call it *knowledge-minimalism*. It has had defenders,[69] and my aim here is to rationally embolden such a stance. This Element has evaluated a substantial body of representative epistemology, in effect asking how well it can guide us beyond knowledge-minimalism. Modalised epistemology, in standard manner, begins by picturing knowledge as at least a true belief. But then, when aiming to describe what to *add* to that picture in order to attain a fuller (and non-minimalist) rendering of knowledge's nature, in fact (even if not consciously) it *leaves behind* that commitment to knowledge's being at least

---

[69] See Sartwell (1991; 1992) and Hetherington (2011a: chapter 4; 2018a; 2018c; 2020), and perhaps Hawthorne (2004: 68–9) on some contexts. On that stark formulation, knowing *is* nothing beyond having a true belief. There have been less-stark formulations: Goldman (1999: 23–6) and I (Hetherington 2001) advocate a hierarchy of epistemically qualitative *grades* of knowing, with mere true belief that p as the lowest possible grade of knowledge that p, for a specific p. Nor do the options end there. Foley (2012) proposes that knowledge is in itself a true belief, if one also has enough important information about the case at hand. His 'information-added' conception threatens to steer us away from a minimalism about knowing's nature. Even here, though, there is a way to remain minimalist. We might treat Foley's core idea as an *essentialist* thesis, saying that a true belief is the *essence* of any instance of knowledge. This is compatible with an *accidentalist* reading of his 'wider' view: knowledge that p is a true belief that p – this much is essential – but in contingent practice, depending on context, further information might be needed, although there is no a priori way to specify *what*, if any, information is needed. (I return to that idea before ending this Element.)

a true belief. In this methodological sense, it *fails* to be adding to the picture with which it began, of knowledge as at least a true belief.

Are there other ways – post-Gettier but non-modalised ones – to conceive of knowledge in a non-minimalist way? Perhaps so. Can this Element's argument be brought to bear upon them, too (*mutatis mutandis*)? We will see. I regard this Element's argument as a small step in a larger project.[70]

In that spirit, here is some explication – and a correlative challenge.

When knowledge-minimalism says that there is nothing more to knowing than the presence of a true belief, I hear this as a metaphysical thesis, describing knowledge's 'inner' nature: literally nothing is involved, in something's being knowledge per se, other than its being a true belief. But I do not infer from this that, as it happens, no instances of knowledge have – in at least the sense of being conjoined with instantiations of – features beyond being true and being a belief. Maybe some do. Maybe all do. My metaphysical reading of knowledge-minimalism is compatible with an 'empirical' non-minimalism about knowledge's 'outer' nature, where this might reflect empirical facts about how knowing is actually manifested in our world. This is why I said 'as it happens' a moment ago: the metaphysical reading is compatible with many, even all, actual instances of knowledge *also* having (even if not in a 'deeply constitutive' way) epistemically valuable, perhaps readily observable, further features, such as being accompanied by good evidence – features to which epistemologists rightly devote much attention. My point is that these further features would never be part of the knowing's *essence as* knowing, being knowledge *at all*. They would be like a person's clothes – yet *without* 'making the person'. They might 'cover' the knowledge, even making it publicly respectable – yet without being literally a constitutive part of it.

Let me expand a little on that metaphysical story (after which, I draw an epistemic implication).

- Suppose, for argument's sake, not only that some, but even that all, actual instances of what we would want to regard as knowing are 'closely accompanied by' further features – epistemic ones – beyond 'true belief'. People readily say, 'This is part of why we value knowing'. Perhaps there is an interesting range of those features, with variability in which instances of knowing are accompanied by which ones. Sometimes, for example, good evidence is consciously present within knowing. At other times, it is absent but there is a compensatory truth-indicative reliability in how the true belief is produced. And so on.

---

[70] A related step, directed at post-Gettier epistemology more generally, occurs elsewhere (Hetherington 2016a).

- Many epistemologists would cite that 'value-adding' kind of story about knowledge as why we should reject knowledge-minimalism, responding to Knowing's Further Features question with a confident 'yes'. After which, energy is devoted to trying to ascertain *which* further features are needed.[71]
- But, again, that usual (non-minimalist) response is metaphysically optional at best. We can apply the distinction between *essence* and *accident* to instances of knowing, along the following lines.

  ○ Knowledge's essence is knowledge per se – knowledge, *strictly* speaking. On knowledge-minimalism, this is *true belief* – nothing more.
  ○ Knowledge's accidents differ from one possible world to another, never part of the knowledge per se – never part of the knowledge itself, strictly speaking.
  ○ Instead, what knowledge's accidents do is to *accompany* the knowledge, without ever being literally *embedded within* it, helping to *constitute* its being knowledge at all.
  ○ In empirical practice, those accidents might well be part of what one *observes* when espying an instance of knowing. In such circumstances, they might even *seem* to be immovably present within the knowledge. This can be why we infer that they are essential to the knowing, hence why we include them in any proposed definition of knowledge.
  ○ But that inference would be invalid. For the presence of those further features can still be metaphysically *extrinsic* to the knowing as such, even when they are accompanying it.
  ○ Specific accidents are thus at most further, metaphysically accidental, features of specific instances of knowledge within a given world. They are not *defining* features of the knowledge per se, not part of why those instances are cases of knowledge *at all*.
  ○ All of that is available to us, once we allow the distinction between essence and accident for instances of knowing.

- Again, I am not denying that such features can bring epistemic *benefits* in their train. Maybe they do make some or all of those instances of knowledge more valuable. Maybe knowledge would never have been valued at all if not for our observing instances of those accidents. Yet being knowledge remains

---

[71] Here we should bear in mind this Element's *critical* reasoning. No matter how 'plausible' or 'intuitive' the value-adding form of story might sound, we have found methodological limitations upon how the story's details could be coherently written. Standard modalised 'further features' are not available even within this conciliatory story. And recall just how extensive is that list of oft-championed features. Not only does it include Nozick's modalised 3 and 4; for example, it includes sensitivity conditions, safety conditions, veritic luck conditions, and maybe more. In short, if knowing has an essence even as minimal as true belief, already there are limits on what accidental features could ever be part of knowing.

one thing; being improved as knowledge, at least in the sense of being knowledge with welcome further features in practice, can be another. That metaphysical distinction can obtain, regardless of whether it is also empirically observable within a specific world. Empirically, we might always find knowing being paired with some form of epistemic justification. Metaphysically, however, that is not enough to establish that knowing always *includes*, in its essential nature, such justification.[72]

And from that metaphysical explication emerges the following epistemic challenge, bearing upon some standard epistemological practices.[73]

How can epistemologists, when insisting on knowing's always, in any possible circumstance, including further epistemic features, know that they are not confusing knowledge's essence with its accidents? How can they know that they are not misreading specific cases in that respect? How can they know that they are not mistaking contingently welcome epistemic aspects of a context or circumstance where knowing is present, for necessarily present features of all possible, hence all actual, instances of knowing?[74]

---

[72] Incidentally, I do not regard this Element as *proving* that knowledge is merely a true belief, or even that its *essence* is merely a true belief. At most, I am suggesting that *if* knowledge has an essence, its essence is true belief. Earlier, though (in notes 40 and 41), I mentioned my having argued elsewhere for a knowledge-practicalism, on which all knowing-that is knowing-how. On that approach, even believing, for example, is not essential to knowing, and truth, even *if* essential, could be present in more than one way: see Hetherington (2019c).

[73] To advert to one debate that can be viewed afresh from this perspective, consider whether knowing that p must include knowing that one knows that p. I am partial to how Matilal (1986: 137–40) uses that distinction when adapting some thinking from Gaṅgeśa, to generate a Nyāya response to the sceptic Śrīharṣa (mentioned earlier), who was arguing against Udayana's conception of knowing. That debate's structure, even if not entirely its substance, coheres with my thinking. (Not entirely its substance, because Nyāya is a *pramāṇa* conception, whereby knowledge is always knowing – an episode resulting from one of a few approved knowing methods.) On my minimalism, what was formerly seen as essential to knowing – namely, justification – can be treated as an inessential-but-often-desirable 'extra'; and one way to think of it is as amounting, when true itself, to *knowledge that* one knows. We thus blend two standard challenges – how to understand justification's nature and role within knowing that p, and how to understand the nature and appeal of knowing that one knows that p.

[74] These questions are intended to evoke, in style and form, some classic *sceptical* doubts. Do you know that you are not dreaming? Do you know that the world is not about to change? And so on. The questions raised just now are meta-epistemological and accordingly might be engaged with in parallel ways to how we might engage with classic (lower-level) sceptical doubts. To take just one example (from a referee), these current questions might be set aside if we envisage epistemological claims, about knowledge's presence or absence, as not even aspiring to being knowledge. Maybe they are more akin to explanatory theories that are not presumed to be knowledge. I am sympathetic to that idea, with its also weakening how confidently epistemologists should express those claims. Similarly, we might not insist on such claims even being full *beliefs*, say (see, e.g., Carter 2018). But bear in mind that, from this Element's outset, we have been discussing a thesis about which even *Socrates* is fully confident, claiming to *know* something about knowledge.

To me, it seems possible that epistemologists have not yet done justice to the challenge behind those questions. Epistemology has long investigated supposed ways in which knowledge would arise, as a step towards establishing whether it can, let alone does, arise: do we gain knowledge through perception, memory, testimony, reason, and so on? That same investigative urgency should also be felt about epistemology's own epistemic powers. In what ways would epistemological knowledge arise? For example, which aspect(s) of epistemological methodology could reveal, with a rational certainty amounting to knowledge, the usual metaphysical conclusion that knowledge's essence is more than true belief?

Consider being assured by an epistemologist that 'intuition', say, reveals to her that knowledge is not merely true belief – even that this is so in any possible world. Does that assurance turn aside the present challenge? I have not grounded my knowledge-minimalist challenge in any 'counter-intuition'; it is grounded in the Element's argument. Was that enough? Or are 'intuitions' enough to deter my argument? Is 'intuition' enough to deliver definitive knowledge of knowledge's inner metaphysical nature – something beyond 'true belief'? Should we dismiss knowledge-minimalism because 'we know by intuition that it is false'? I do not believe so. Being assured of knowledge-minimalism's 'counter-intuitive' nature is epistemically inconclusive at best.[75] Dismissing a view because it is 'counter-intuitive', as can occur, would seem to reflect a confidence that philosophy is *easier* than most of us usually *say* it is.[76]

7.2 A Final Word – from Socrates?

And that is where I would have ended this Element, if not for a remarkable discovery.

A few months ago, fossicking in a deeply dusty Sydney bookshop, I found, inside another volume, what appear to be a few *further* pages from the *Theaetetus* – a brief continuation of it. Strikingly, they seem to show Socrates guiding us towards knowledge-minimalism. It is generally said that the dialogue ends aporetically, reaching no definition of knowledge. Yet might these new pages point in a contrary direction? They make apparent how easily Socrates'

---

[75] So too (I concede) is this paragraph's somewhat polemical style and casual tone! I acknowledge that epistemologists often surround their uses of 'intuition' with sophisticated discussions of such matters as social roles of knowing (rather than true belief), potential links between knowing and such actions as assertion, and so on. For influential accounts along those lines, see especially Craig (1990) and Williamson (2000).

[76] Personally, I share Ballantyne's (2019: 301) sense that, within the drama that is philosophy's entirety, each of us is 'an extra'. Nothing less than that, since at least we are on the stage, uttering our lines, being heard right now; but nothing more than that, with no assurance of continuing to be heard beyond this moment.

line of argument *can* be turned into support for a definition of knowledge, albeit not the form of definition that most of us would have expected to meet.[77]

Here are those extra pages (along with what, in my enthusiasm, I call their *Stephen* page numbering – inspired by, and following, the dialogue's official Stephanus numbering).

210e THEODORUS. Tomorrow, then, Socrates.

THEAETETUS. From me, too, farewell.

SOCR. A moment, Theaetetus; perhaps I spoke too hastily just now, of 'mere wind-eggs'. I alluded to your 'having the good sense not to fancy you know what you do not know'. Earlier, we had agreed on knowledge's being something beyond a mere true belief. That was clearly true, we thought. But were we correct? Or was even *that* easy to say, yet not to know? I am struck by a new idea. You have heard of what some call the paradox of inquiry, or of the learner?

211a. THEAET. I have.

SOCR. Let us blend it with our thinking from a moment ago, when we were setting aside our third and final proposal as to the nature of a *logos*, a proposal arising in our attempt to define knowledge.

THEAET. Do you have more to say on this, Socrates?

SOCR. I do. And I welcome your patience with an old man, helping me to inquire. The paradox arose for me in a conversation that I once enjoyed with Meno. It can be stated with the following words (although they are not what I recall using).[78] 'To seek knowledge about some specific thing, a person must in some sense know the specific

b. thing already for this to be the thing about which knowledge is sought. And to achieve articulate knowledge about a specific object, a person must know what the thing is already to recognize this as the thing about which knowledge is to be gained. In its most general form, the problem is to explain how knowledge is possible originally, inasmuch as gaining knowledge requires something previously known.'

THEAET. Those are insightful words, Socrates.

---

[77] As Rowett (2018: 252 n. 68) reminds us (and as was mentioned in note 21), some philosophers regard the *Theaetetus* as ending by 'hinting at analysis that would come close to succeeding (something like JTB). Many think the third meaning of "account" promising or nearly perfect, and some see a hint that analysis by collection and division (as in the *Sophist* etc.) is the way forward.' Section 6.4 discussed the latter approach. But if we see only the more generic former idea – an endorsement of JTB – as still 'in the air' at the dialogue's end, the argument we are about to meet undermines even *that* idea.

[78] Here I must record my amazement, since these quoted words appear also in a contemporary book, from Sayre (2005: 189). Yet I know – I would stake my life on this – that Sayre never saw these Stephen pages from the *Theaetetus*.

c. Socr. Yours in return are words of kindness, Theaetetus. I mention the paradox because it seems to strengthen the argument that has prompted our moving away from our third proposal for the nature of *logos*. So much so, that . . . well, let us see.

Theaet. What are you envisaging, Socrates?

Socr. I will tell you, Theaetetus, although slowly. Care is needed, given what is at stake. I am now wondering whether we can *ever* understand knowledge as something more than true belief.

d. Theaet. I am intrigued, Socrates – and a little worried. Knowledge *must* be more than true belief. We know this, if anything, about knowledge.

Socr. I also hope not to lose that confidence, Theaetetus. Let me take hold of my thoughts, so as to examine them thoroughly.

Theaet. I am eager to know them.

Socr. We can develop them in two stages, initially with our third suggested description of *logos*, then in more general terms.

Theaet. That is a sensible plan.

e. Socr. Thank you, Theaetetus. Our third suggestion described a *logos* as a *distinguishing mark*. To know X, we proposed, one must have in mind a mark distinguishing X from any other thing, any non-X Y. But two interlinked problems appeared.

Theaet. Indeed they did.

Socr. We agreed that to think of the mark in that way – as revealing where X ends, so to speak, and any Y begins – is already to think of X, as something with a boundary, thus described, between it and any given Y. More than that, this thinking of X would be knowledge. We would already know enough about X to know that the mark, in whatever other terms it is being described, is sufficient for marking off X from any Y.

Theaet. Yes, that was the first problem, Socrates.

212a. Socr. We therefore considered an alternative description of the mark, so that we were not already knowing X in knowing its mark. We would still need to know the mark itself, though. Hence, we could regard ourselves as knowing X only by crediting ourselves with that further knowledge. And this is not a description of how knowing is constituted *at all* – in this case, the knowledge of X, but really *any* knowledge, since 'X' is anything at all. We would be failing to understand how *any* true belief within us could become knowledge, thanks to the addition of a *logos*, on the picture of *logos* painted by our third proposal.

b. Theaet. That was our difficulty, Socrates. I saw no escape from it, other than our happening, on a future occasion, upon an *improved* description of the nature of *logos*. This was where we were about to leave the matter, were we not?

SOCR. Alas, Theaetetus, even that thought of a possible future escape from this thinking might be false. Will you please bear with me a moment longer as I say more about this?

THEAET. Gladly, Socrates.

SOCR. Our topic was the idea of a distinguishing mark being a *logos*. I will now use abbreviations. We were considering *DM serving as L*. That is, in trying to understand the nature of a *logos* (as an addition to TD – true *doxa* – when understanding what else is needed for creating knowledge), we proposed *distinguishing mark* as a specific description of the generic idea of *logos*.[79]

c. Let us reverse that, in our new thinking. We will consider *L serving as DM*. In other words, we may peruse the generic idea of adding a *logos at all* to a TD (regardless of how we might wish to describe *logos* in more specific terms), so as to bring knowledge into existence. We are asking whether *some* form of L can be a DM at all.

THEAET. I understand this shift of focus, Socrates.

SOCR. I knew that you would, Theaetetus. Next we add further details.

THEAET. I am attending closely.

SOCR. We adapt our previous reasoning, applying it to this new description.

THEAET. How so, Socrates?

SOCR. Previously we were asking about knowledge of some X. Now we turn that talk of 'X' into talk of *knowledge itself*. We might describe it as *what knowledge is*. And we apply afresh our previous reasoning, directing it at the proposal *that some L is itself a DM*, when what needs to be created (courtesy of that L being a DM) is our

d. knowing *what knowledge is*.

THEAET. That is what we are seeking to understand. I see.

SOCR. Yes, we adapt, for this instance, our earlier reasoning. It had two parts. Here was the first, in our current terms. To describe some DM for X (with the DM being an L needed) for knowing X is *already* to have described X fully enough, so that describing the DM adds nothing

---

[79] Here, I have taken the liberty of using 'DM' to accord with the English-language term 'distinguishing mark'. The main Greek word used in the earlier Stephanus pages (and in these Stephen pages, too) is *sēmeion* – 'sign' or 'stamp'. For discussion of the resonances in these uses, see Giannopoulou (2013: 175–7) and Rowett (2018: 252–4). Note also that here I stay with Socrates' word '*doxa*'. Elsewhere, for simplicity, I have not questioned the epistemologically standard translation of this as 'belief', even though it is possibly not an ideal translation for Socrates' thinking (Moss and Schwab 2019). Moss (2021) reinforces that point about '*doxa*', and extends it, *mutatis mutandis*, to the word '*epistēmē*' and its epistemologically standard translation as 'knowledge'.

towards portraying X – the portrayal already present, by hypothesis, in one's TD of X. Hence, describing the DM adds nothing about X that is not *already* sufficiently present in the TD of X. If knowledge of X is present after adding the DM, therefore, this is because such knowledge was *already* present.

e. THEAET. Yes, that was it. That was our earlier reasoning's first half.

SOCR. Here is how we adapt it now. To describe some L (as a DM needed) for knowing *what knowledge is* is already to have described *what knowledge is*, fully enough to amount already to knowing *what knowledge is*. Hence, describing some L (serving as a DM) adds nothing towards knowing *what knowledge is*, nothing that is not already sufficiently present to amount already to knowing *what knowledge is*.

THEAET. That seems so.

SOCR. Now add a detail. In the reasoning's previous version, we did not have in mind a specific description of X, to which we were adding a specific DM, since 'X' was wholly general. But in our reasoning's new version, we do start from a specific description. We are discussing whether describing *some L* (serving as a DM) adds anything needed to TD if we are to understand knowing *what knowledge is*. You see,

213a. Theaetetus, how our earlier reasoning, once we extend its reach, threatens to return us to saying that 'TD' *is* already a sufficient description of knowing *what knowledge is*.

THEAET. So far, that is true. Can we escape it this time?

SOCR. I do not think so. For the second half of our earlier form of argument may likewise be adapted.

THEAET. I do not yet see this.

SOCR. That second half, in its earlier form, called it 'a pretty business', you might recall, to claim that *knowing* some DM (serving as an L) is part of how knowing X could arise (for any 'X'). For this would be to claim to understand some knowledge (of the 'any' X) partly in terms of other knowledge (this time, of DM). Hence, one would fail to explain how knowledge *at all* can ever arise, and thereby to explain the nature of knowing, even partly in terms of some DM (serving as an L).

b. THEAET. I recall well that part of our prior reasoning.

SOCR. Here is how easily it applies to our present case. To claim that *knowing* some L (serving as a DM) is a needed element in knowing *what knowledge is* (here we are again letting 'X' be 'what knowledge is') is likewise 'a pretty business', since this is to describe some knowledge (of *what knowledge is*) partly in terms of other knowledge (of some L). Hence, one is failing to explain how knowledge *at all* could ever arise, and thereby to explain the nature of knowing, even partly in terms of some L (serving as a DM). And, as I added a moment ago, since this time the L (which is any possible L) is supposedly acting as a DM between *true belief* and *what knowledge is*, we find ourselves with this conclusion: we cannot

c. know any L to *be* a DM, distinguishing *what knowledge is* from *true belief*. We cannot know any *logos* to be a distinguishing mark between true belief and knowledge.

THEAET. I am stunned, Socrates. I must gather my breath. Does this really place us where I fear that it does, in our attempt to understand what knowing is?

SOCR. Fear is not needed, Theaetetus. But care is, along with a sincere welcoming of whatever presents itself as true, upon reasoned examination.

THEAET. That is so, Socrates, as always.

SOCR. It does seem that we should retract what, formerly, we had been so quick to accept – that a belief's being true is not sufficient for its being knowledge. We must not remain so confident in this view of knowledge. It might not be correct. Day to day, when seeking knowledge, maybe we encounter instances of it with accompanying characteristics that can

d. change from day to day, much as you and I today wear this, and tomorrow wear that, item of clothing. Just as you and I, however, remain the same people that we are, even throughout changes of clothing, any instance of knowing in its defining nature, *what it is* in being knowledge at all, is ... well, as I said, perhaps it is nothing beyond a true belief. Maybe *logos*, when present along with knowing, is simply *clothing*. It is usually welcome. It is needed in most settings. But it is not even part of what *makes* knowledge knowledge. Clothes are not even part of what *makes* the man. Nor, equally, does *logos* make the knowledge.

e. THEAET. I am struck, as ever, Socrates, by the agility of your thinking. I must, also as ever, learn from your example.

SOCR. I appreciate such generous words, my young friend. Now I *must* hasten away, presumably to listen to some less generous words.

Is Socrates correct in these formerly lost words of his? I cannot say so with full confidence. Still, he was a remarkably wise man, was he not? Of course, his reasoning here might not be flawless. Then again, whose is?

What does flow from these newly discovered words is the thought that maybe Socrates, at least, should withdraw his earlier claim in the *Theaetetus*

(201a–c) to know that knowledge is something more than true *doxa* – true belief. This was among the few claims to knowledge, we saw, that he was ever willing to make. And now? Perhaps even that thesis about knowledge – no matter that it *seemed* to him, as it does to many, to be clearly true – is no longer something that he should have claimed to know.

This does not prove knowledge-minimalism's truth. But it does strengthen the case at least a little for adopting that view of knowledge – for thinking that knowledge might, in its essential 'inner' nature, be nothing beyond true belief. If nothing else, we should be prompted to examine this issue more thoroughly. This is a complex matter. It has methodological and metaphysical aspects barely touched upon in many current reflections on knowledge's nature. How reassuring it is to read Socrates, in these freshly found pages, doing further justice to those aspects.

References

Anderson, C. (2019). The Gettier problem and fallibilism. In S. Hetherington, ed., *The Gettier Problem*, Cambridge: Cambridge University Press, pp. 11–26.

Ballantyne, N. (2019). *Knowing Our Limits*, New York: Oxford University Press.

Becker, K. and Black, T., eds. (2012). *The Sensitivity Principle in Epistemology*, Cambridge: Cambridge University Press.

Beddor, B. and Goldstein, S. (in press). Mighty knowledge. *Journal of Philosophy*.

Beddor, B. and Pavese, C. (2020). Modal virtue epistemology. *Philosophy and Phenomenological Research*, 101: 61–79.

Benson, H. H. (2013). The priority of definition. In J. Bussanich and N. D. Smith, eds., *The Bloomsbury Companion to Socrates*, London: Bloomsbury, pp. 136–55, 342–7.

Bjelde, J. (2021). Knowledge is teachable. *Mind*, 130: 475–502.

Bluck, R. S., ed. (1961). *Plato's* Meno, Cambridge: Cambridge University Press.

Bogardus, T. and Perrin, W. (2022). Knowledge is believing something because it's true. *Episteme*, 19: 178–96.

Bostock, D. (1988). *Plato's* Theaetetus, Oxford: Clarendon Press.

Bradley, B. (2009). *Well-Being and Death*, Oxford: Clarendon Press.

Bronstein, D. (2016). *Aristotle on Knowledge and Learning: The* Posterior Analytics, Oxford: Oxford University Press.

Brown, J. (2018). *Fallibilism: Evidence and Knowledge*, Oxford: Oxford University Press.

Burnyeat, M. (1990). Introduction. In M. J. Levett, trans., *The* Theaetetus *of Plato*, Indianapolis: Hackett, pp. 1–241.

Carter, J. A. (2018). On behalf of controversial view agnosticism. *European Journal of Philosophy*, 26: 1358–70.

Carter, J. A. and Bondy, P., eds. (2020). *Well-Founded Belief: New Essays on the Epistemic Basing Relation*, New York: Routledge.

Cassam, Q. (2009). Can the concept of knowledge be analysed? In P. Greenough and D. Pritchard, eds., *Williamson on Knowledge*, Oxford: Oxford University Press, pp. 12–30.

Chalmers, D. J. (2012). *Constructing the World*, Oxford: Oxford University Press.

Corlett. J. A. (2005). *Interpreting Plato's Dialogues*, Las Vegas: Parmenides Publishing.

Cornford, F. M. (1935). *Plato's Theory of Knowledge: The* Theaetetus *and the* Sophist *of Plato Translated with a Running Commentary*, London: Routledge & Kegan Paul.

Cottingham, J., Stoothoff, R., and Murdoch, D., trans. (1985). *The Philosophical Writings of Descartes*, vol. 1, Cambridge: Cambridge University Press.

Craig, E. (1990). *Knowledge and the State of Nature: An Essay in Conceptual Synthesis*, Oxford: Clarendon Press.

Dancy, J. (1985). *An Introduction to Contemporary Epistemology*, Oxford: Blackwell.

Deslauriers, M. (2007). *Aristotle on Definition*, Leiden: Brill.

Dougherty, T. (2011). Fallibilism. In S. Bernecker and D. Pritchard, eds., *The Routledge Companion to Epistemology*, New York: Routledge, pp. 131–43.

Dretske, F. (1970). Epistemic operators. *Journal of Philosophy*, 67: 1007–23.

Dretske, F. (1971). Conclusive reasons. *Australasian Journal of Philosophy*, 49: 1–22.

Engel, M. (1992). Is epistemic luck compatible with knowledge? *Southern Journal of Philosophy*, 30: 59–75.

Engel, M. (2011). Epistemic luck. In J. Fieser and B. Dowden, eds., *Internet Encyclopedia of Philosophy*. www.iep.utm.edu/epi-luck.

Fine, G. (1979). Knowledge and *logos* in the *Theaetetus*. *Philosophical Review*, 88: 366–97.

Fischer, J. M. and Ravizza, M. (1998). *Responsibility and Control: A Theory of Moral Responsibility*, Cambridge: Cambridge University Press.

Foley, R. (2012). *When Is True Belief Knowledge?* Princeton: Princeton University Press.

Frankfurt, H. (1969). Alternate possibilities and moral responsibility, *Journal of Philosophy*, 66: 829–39.

Ganeri, J. (2017). Śrīharṣa's dissident epistemology: Of knowledge as assurance. In J. Ganeri, ed., *The Oxford Handbook of Indian Philosophy*, Oxford: Oxford University Press, pp. 522–38.

Gerson, L. P. (2009). *Ancient Epistemology*, Cambridge: Cambridge University Press.

Gettier, E. L. (1963). Is justified true belief knowledge? *Analysis*, 23: 121–3.

Giannopoulou, Z. (2013). *Plato's* Theaetetus *as a Second* Apology, Oxford: Oxford University Press.

Glock, H.-J. (2008). *What Is Analytic Philosophy?* Cambridge: Cambridge University Press.

Goldman, A. I. (1999). *Knowledge in a Social World*, Oxford: Clarendon Press.

Greco, J. (2003). Knowledge as credit for true belief. In M. DePaul and L. Zagzebski, eds., *Intellectual Virtue: Perspectives from Ethics and Epistemology*, New York: Oxford University Press, pp. 111–34.

Greco, J. (2010). *Achieving Knowledge: A Virtue-Theoretic Account of Epistemic Normativity*, Cambridge: Cambridge University Press.

Greco, J. (2012). A (different) virtue epistemology. *Philosophy and Phenomenological Research*, 85: 1–26.

Grube, G. M. A., trans. (1981). *Plato: Five Dialogues*, Indianapolis: Hackett Publishing.

Gunderson, L. B. (2003). *Dispositional Theories of Knowledge: A Defence of Aetiological Foundationalism*, Aldershot: Ashgate Publishing.

Hales, S. D. (2020). *The Myth of Luck: Philosophy, Fate, and Fortune*, London: Bloomsbury Academic.

Hamilton, E. and Cairns, H., eds. (1961). *Plato: The Collected Dialogues*, Princeton: Princeton University Press.

Hawthorne, J. (2004). *Knowledge and Lotteries*, Oxford: Clarendon Press.

Hetherington, S. (1996). *Knowledge Puzzles: An Introduction to Epistemology*, Boulder:Westview Press.

Hetherington, S. (1999). Knowing failably. *Journal of Philosophy*, 96: 565–87.

Hetherington, S. (2001). *Good Knowledge, Bad Knowledge: On Two Dogmas of Epistemology*, Oxford: Clarendon Press.

Hetherington, S. (2011a). *How to Know: A Practicalist Conception of Knowing*, Malden, MA: Wiley-Blackwell.

Hetherington, S. (2011b). Knowledge and knowing: Ability and manifestation. In S. Tolksdorf, ed., *Conceptions of Knowledge*, Berlin: De Gruyter, pp. 73–100.

Hetherington, S. (2011c). The Gettier problem. In S. Bernecker and D. Pritchard, eds., *The Routledge Companion to Epistemology*, New York: Routledge, pp. 119–30.

Hetherington, S. (2014). Knowledge can be lucky. In M. Steup, J. Turri, and E. Sosa, eds., *Contemporary Debates in Epistemology*, 2nd ed., Malden: Wiley Blackwell, pp. 164–76.

Hetherington, S. (2016a). *Knowledge and the Gettier Problem*, Cambridge: Cambridge University Press.

Hetherington, S. (2016b). Understanding fallible warrant and fallible knowledge: Three proposals. *Pacific Philosophical Quarterly*, 97: 270–82.

Hetherington, S. (2017a). Gettier cases: Transworld identity and counterparts. In R. Borges, C. de Almeida, and P. Klein, eds., *Explaining Knowledge: New Essays on the Gettier Problem*, Oxford: Oxford University Press, pp. 366–83.

Hetherington, S. (2017b). Knowledge as potential for action. *European Journal of Pragmatism and American Philosophy*, 9. https://doi.org/10.4000/ejpap.1070.

Hetherington, S. (2018a). Knowing as simply being correct. In B. Zhang and S. Tong, eds., *A Dialogue between Law and Philosophy: Proceedings of the International Conference on Facts and Evidence*, Beijing: Chinese University of Political Science and Law Press, pp. 68–82.

Hetherington, S. (2018b). Knowledge and knowledge-claims: Austin and beyond. In S. L. Tsohatzidis, ed., *Interpreting Austin: Critical Essays*, Cambridge: Cambridge University Press, pp. 206–22.

Hetherington, S. (2018c). The redundancy problem: From knowledge-infallibilism to knowledge-minimalism. *Synthese*, 195: 4683–702.

Hetherington, S. (2019a). *What Is Epistemology?* Cambridge: Polity.

Hetherington, S. (2019b). Conceiving of knowledge in modal terms? In S. Hetherington and M. Valaris, eds., *The Philosophy of Knowledge: A History*, vol. 4, *Knowledge in Contemporary Philosophy*, London: Bloomsbury, pp. 231–48.

Hetherington, S. (2019c). Creating the world: God's knowledge as power. *Suri*, 8: 1–18.

Hetherington, S. (2020a). Knowledge as skill. In E. Fridland and C. Pavese, eds., *The Routledge Handbook of Philosophy of Skill and Expertise*, New York: Routledge, pp. 168–78.

Hetherington, S. (2020b). Knowledge-minimalism: Reinterpreting Plato's *Meno* on knowledge and true belief. In S. Hetherington and N. D. Smith, eds., *What the Ancients Offer to Contemporary Epistemology*, New York: Routledge, pp. 25–40.

Hetherington, S. (in press a). Knowing can include luck. In B. Roeber, E. Sosa, M. Steup, and J. Turri, eds. *Contemporary Debates in Epistemology*, 3rd ed., Malden, MA: Wiley-Blackwell.

Hetherington, S. (in press b). On whether knowing can include luck: Asking the correct question. In B. Roeber, E. Sosa, M. Steup, and J. Turri, eds. *Contemporary Debates in Epistemology*, 3rd ed., Malden, MA: Wiley-Blackwell.

Jowett, B., trans. (1931 [1892]). *The Dialogues of Plato*, 3rd edn, Oxford: Clarendon Press.

Kaplan, M. (1985). It's not what you know that counts. *Journal of Philosophy*, 82: 350–63.

Kelp, C. (2013). Knowledge: The safe-apt view. *Australasian Journal of Philosophy*, 91: 265–78.

Kirkham, R. L. (1984). Does the Gettier problem rest on a mistake? *Mind*, 93: 501–13.

Kornblith, H. (2002). *Knowledge and its Place in Nature*, Oxford: Clarendon Press.

Kornblith, H. (2006). Appeals to intuition and the ambition of epistemology. In S. Hetherington, ed., *Epistemology Futures*, Oxford: Clarendon Press, pp. 10–25.

Lackey, J. (2007). Why we don't deserve credit for everything we know. *Synthese* 158: 345–61.

Lennox, J. G., trans. and comm. (2001). *Aristotle*: On the Parts of Animals, Oxford: Clarendon Press.

Lewis, D. (1973). *Counterfactuals*, Oxford: Basil Blackwell.

Lewis, D. (1983). Introduction. In his *Philosophical Papers*, Vol. 1, New York: Oxford University Press, pp. ix–xi.

Luper-Foy, S., ed. (1987). *The Possibility of Knowledge: Nozick and his Critics*, Totowa, NJ: Rowman & Littlefield.

Lycan, W. G. (2006). On the Gettier problem problem. In S. Hetherington, ed., *Epistemology Futures*, Oxford: Clarendon Press, pp. 148–68.

Matilal, B. K. (1986). *Perception: An Essay on Classical Indian Theories of Knowledge*, Oxford: Clarendon Press.

McDowell, J., trans. (1973). *Plato*: Theaetetus, Oxford: Clarendon Press.

McEvilley, T. (2002). *The Shape of Ancient Thought: Comparative Studies in Greek and Indian Philosophies*, New York: Allworth Press.

McKeon, R. M., ed. (1941). *The Basic Works of Aristotle*, New York: Random House.

Morrow, G. R., trans. and comm. (1962). *Plato's Epistles*, Indianapolis, IN: Bobbs-Merrill.

Moss, J. (2021). *Plato's Epistemology: Being and Seeming*, Oxford: Oxford University Press.

Moss, J. and Schwab, W. (2019). The birth of belief. *Journal of the History of Philosophy*, 57: 1–32.

Nails, D. (2006). The life of Plato of Athens. In H. H. Benson, ed., *A Companion to Plato*, Malden, MA: Blackwell, pp. 1–12.

Nozick, R. (1981). *Philosophical Explanations*, Cambridge, MA: Harvard University Press.

Plantinga, A. (1993a). *Warrant: The Current Debate*, New York: Oxford University Press.

Plantinga, A. (1993b). *Warrant and Proper Function*, New York: Oxford University Press.

Prior, W. J. (2006). The Socratic problem. In H.H. Benson, ed., *A Companion to Plato*, Malden, MA: Blackwell, pp. 25–35.

Pritchard, D. (2005). *Epistemic Luck*, Oxford: Clarendon Press.

Pritchard, D. (2007). Anti-luck epistemology. *Synthese*, 158: 277–97.

Pritchard, D. (2008). Sensitivity, safety, and antiluck epistemology. In J. Greco, ed., *The Oxford Handbook of Skepticism*, New York: Oxford University Press, pp. 437–55.

Pritchard, D. (2012). Anti-luck virtue epistemology. *Journal of Philosophy*, 109: 247–79.

Pritchard, D. (2014). Knowledge cannot be lucky. In M. Steup, J. Turri, and E. Sosa, eds., *Contemporary Debates in Epistemology*, 2nd ed., Malden, MA: Wiley Blackwell, pp. 152–64.

Pritchard, S. (2020). Anti-risk virtue epistemology. In C. Kelp and J. Greco, eds., *Virtue Theoretic Epistemology: New Methods and Approaches*, Cambridge: Cambridge University Press, pp. 203–24

Reed, B. (2002). How to think about fallibilism. *Philosophical Studies*, 107: 143–57.

Robinson, R. (1971). Socratic definition. In G. Vlastos, ed., *The Philosophy of Socrates: A Collection of Critical Essays*, Garden City: Anchor Books, pp. 110–24.

Roush, S. (2005). *Tracking Truth: Knowledge, Evidence, and Science*, Oxford: Clarendon Press.

Rowett, C. (2018). *Knowledge and Truth in Plato: Stepping Past the Shadow of Socrates*, Oxford: Oxford University Press.

Sartwell, C. (1991). Knowledge is merely true belief. *American Philosophical Quarterly*, 28: 157–65.

Sartwell, C. (1992). Why knowledge is merely true belief. *Journal of Philosophy*, 89: 167–80.

Sayre, K. M. (1969). *Plato's Analytic Method*, Chicago: University of Chicago Press.

Sayre, K. M. (1995). *Plato's Literary Garden: How to Read a Platonic Dialogue*, Notre Dame, IN: University of Notre Dame Press.

Sayre, K. M. (2005). *Plato's Late Ontology: A Riddle Resolved*, 2nd ed., Las Vegas: Parmenides Publishing.

Schwab, W. (2015). Explanation in the epistemology of the *Meno*. *Oxford Studies in Ancient Philosophy*, 48: 1–36.

Scott, D. (2006). *Plato's* Meno, Cambridge: Cambridge University Press.

Shope, R. K. (1983). *The Analysis of Knowing: A Decade of Research*, Princeton: Princeton University Press.

Sosa, E. (1999). How must knowledge be modally related to what is known? *Philosophical Topics*, 26: 373–84.

Sosa, E. (2007). *A Virtue Epistemology: Apt Belief and Reflective Knowledge*, vol. 1, Oxford: Clarendon Press.

Sosa, E. (2011). *Knowing Full Well*, Princeton: Princeton University Press.

Sosa, E. (2015). *Judgment and Agency*, Oxford: Oxford University Press.

Sosa, E. (2016). Knowledge in action. In A. Bahr and M. Seidel, eds., *Ernest Sosa: Targeting his Philosophy*, Dordrecht: Springer, pp. 1–13.

Sosa, E. (2017). *Epistemology*, Princeton: Princeton University Press.

Stalnaker, R.C. (1968). A theory of conditionals. In N. Rescher, ed., *Studies in Logical Theory*, Oxford: Basil Blackwell, pp. 98–112.

Stoltz, J. (2007). Gettier and factivity in Indo-Tibetan epistemology. *Philosophical Quarterly*, 57: 394–415.

Tiles, M. and Tiles, J. (1993). *An Introduction to Historical Epistemology: The Authority of Knowledge*, Oxford: Blackwell.

Todd, W. (1964). Counterfactual conditionals and the presuppositions of induction. *Philosophy of Science*, 31: 101–10.

Turri, J. (2011). Manifest failure: The Gettier problem solved. *Philosophers' Imprint*, 11: 8 (April): 1–11.

Turri, J. (2019 [2012]). In Gettier's wake. In S. Hetherington, ed., *Epistemology: The Key Thinkers*, 2nd ed., London: Bloomsbury, pp. 263–80.

Waterfield, R., trans. (2008). *Plato*: Timaeus *and* Critias, Oxford: Oxford University Press.

Weinberg, J. M., Nichols, S., and Stich, S. (2001). Normativity and epistemic intuitions. *Philosophical Topics*, 29: 429–60.

White, N.P. (1976). *Plato on Knowledge and Reality*, Indianapolis: Hackett Publishing.

White, N.P (1992). Plato's metaphysical epistemology. In R. Kraut, ed., *The Cambridge Companion to Plato*, Cambridge: Cambridge University Press, pp. 277–310.

Williamson, T. (2000). *Knowledge and Its Limits*, Oxford: Clarendon Press.

Williamson, T. (2009). Probability and danger. *The Amherst Lecture in Philosophy* 4: 1–35.

Williamson, T. (2018). *Doing Philosophy: From Common Curiosity to Logical Reasoning*, Oxford: Oxford University Press.

Zagzebski, L. (1996). *Virtues of the Mind: An Inquiry into the Nature of Virtue and the Ethical Foundations of Knowledge*, Cambridge: Cambridge University Press.

Zagzebski, L. (1999). What is knowledge? In J. Greco and E. Sosa, eds., *The Blackwell Guide to Epistemology*, Malden, MA: Blackwell, pp. 92–116.

Zagzebski, L. (2009). *On Epistemology*, Belmont: Wadsworth.

Acknowledgements

I am grateful for extremely helpful comments, on respective drafts of this Element, by David Bronstein, and by two referees for Cambridge University Press. I have welcomed the opportunity to contribute in this way to the Elements in Epistemology series. I was honoured to have been invited to be Editor of the series, which sits within Cambridge University Press's array of Elements series. That editorial opportunity was welcome because I believe in the potency of pithy philosophy. I hope that this Element satisfies that description.

Cambridge Elements ☰

Epistemology

Stephen Hetherington
University of New South Wales, Sydney

Stephen Hetherington is Professor Emeritus of Philosophy at the University of New South Wales, Sydney. He is the author of numerous books including *Knowledge and the Gettier Problem* (Cambridge University Press, 2016) and *What Is Epistemology?* (Polity, 2019), and is the editor of, most recently, *Knowledge in Contemporary Epistemology* (with Markos Valaris: Bloomsbury, 2019), and *What the Ancients Offer to Contemporary Epistemology* (with Nicholas D. Smith: Routledge, 2020). He was the Editor-in-Chief of the *Australasian Journal of Philosophy* from 2013 until 2022.

About the Series

This Elements series seeks to cover all aspects of a rapidly evolving field including emerging and evolving topics such as these: fallibilism; knowing-how; self-knowledge; knowledge of morality; knowledge and injustice; formal epistemology; knowledge and religion; scientific knowledge; collective epistemology; applied epistemology; virtue epistemology; wisdom. The series will demonstrate the liveliness and diversity of the field, pointing also to new areas of investigation.

Cambridge Elements ≡

Epistemology

Elements in the Series

Foundationalism
Richard Fumerton

The Epistemic Consequences of Paradox
Bryan Frances

Coherentism
Erik J. Olsson

The A Priori *Without Magic*
Jared Warren

Defining Knowledge: Method and Metaphysics
Stephen Hetherington

A full series listing is available at: www.cambridge.org/EEPI